DATE DUE

NOV 2 0 2006	
JAN 0 2 2007	
JAN 2 3 2007	
FEB 0 5 2007	
FEB 2 3 2007	
MAR 01 2007	
FEB 0 2 2008	
MAR 0 1 2008	
JUL 2 9 2009 ILL	
MAR 0 8 2010	
OCT 3 0 2013	
NOV 1 9 2013	
FEB 2 7 2016	

GAYLORD   PRINTED IN U.S.A.

Havana
Salsa

Havana salsa

Stories and Recipes

VIVIANA CARBALLO

ATRIA BOOKS

New York   London   Toronto   Sydney

1230 Avenue of the Americas
New York, NY 10020

Library of Congress Cataloging-in-Publication Data

Carballo, Viviana.
    Havana salsa : stories and recipes / Viviana Carballo.
      p. cm.
    ISBN 0-7432-9346-0 (ebook)
      1. Cookery, Cuban. 2. Food habits—Cuba—Havana. 3. Havana (Cuba)—Social life and
customs. 4. Carballo, Viviana. I. Title.

TX716.C9C37 2006
641.597291—dc22

                                                                    2006042905

ISBN 13: 978-0-7432-8516-2
ISBN 10:   0-7432-8516-6

First Atria Books hardcover edition August 2006

10 9 8 7 6 5 4 3 2 1

ATRIA BOOKS is a trademark of Simon & Schuster, Inc.

Manufactured in the United States of America
Designed by Karolina Harris

For information regarding special discounts for bulk purchases, please contact Simon & Schuster
Special Sales at 1-800-456-6798 or business@simonandschuster.com.

To Havana

for what it was

Contents

Note from the Author

All recipes yield 4 to 6 servings unless otherwise indicated.
All butter is unsalted.
All garlic is pressed with a garlic press or minced.
All chorizo is Spanish chorizo, fully cooked.
Piquillo peppers, a Spanish product, are a bit smoky and spicy and come canned or bottled.

Introduction

Let me make clear that this book is neither a dance manual nor a Cuban cookbook per se. And if you are looking for new dance steps or an old black bean recipe you won't find them here. What you will discover is a remembrance of the Havana that was and the food we ate before the Castro catastrophe. *Havana Salsa* is a group of connected stories, all absolutely true, at least 98 percent of the time. With some name changes and to the best of my recollection. The remaining 2 percent consists of a pinch of fantasy and a dash of sentimentality. Much like life itself.

This book has been rattling in my head since Mrs. Prieto, my first-grade teacher at Ruston Academy in Havana, told me I had either a very vivid imagination or a very remarkable family and that, in either case, I should someday write about it.

As time passed things all around me got even more "interesting" and as I retold the stories they seemed harder and harder to believe. But the truth is that my reality was magical in itself; the Havana of the forties and fifties, with its corruption, turbulent politics, delicious decadence, and my eccentric family, is indeed, the stuff of myths.

Born in 1939, I grew up in the Cuba of the forties, when magical realism was first being defined. We may not have recognized the concept in our daily lives, but we were living it—the fusion of the real and the fantastic. A Catholic country famous for its decadence, our Cuba was shaped by opposing perspectives—one rational, the other supernatural. With the continual social and political upheaval, the endless struggle for a political ideal, and the reality of a revolution, the extraordinary was taking place in our lives every day.

The Cuba I knew in pre-Castro days has disappeared, a place in time and space that will never be again.

Cuba now is filled with sadness, crumbling buildings, an agriculture in ruins, an economy in shambles. Long gone are the days filled with music and laughter, the closeness of family now obliterated by a diaspora that started in the early sixties and continues to this day. The sense of humor, the very lust for life that defined the Cuban character, has given way to emotional depletion and a life of extraordinary hardship. Cuba has become a third-world country with little available food, power outages, and water stoppages every day. This is not the Cuba I knew.

Wanting to pass on the mythical quality of my country and that of those around me, I decided to write down my own Cuban history.

At every family gathering, inevitably centered around food, my U.S.-born nephews and nieces ask me to tell them stories of the Cuba I lived in. They know the historical facts as taught in school; they know the politics from reading the papers; they know the traditional food trapped in the fifties' nostalgia of the popular Cuban restaurants in Miami, but the smells, the tastes, the sounds, the soul, the physical feel of the country—that Cuba—they only know through my generation's memories.

Essentially this book is a collection of those stories about my family, a rather eccentric group who conducted their lives against the extraordinary backdrop of Havana. This is a snapshot of who we were and the way we ate with the people we loved. And since there is no bigger cultural trigger than food, the book is set up as a series of vignettes showcasing the food and recipes I associate with each family memory, beginning with my childhood in the forties through the sensual fifties and then the first eighteen months of the Revolution. Havana Salsa tells the history of Havana, my Havana, through the sortilege of its food and the mirror of my family.

When my parents met in the late thirties, they were both married to others, but the difficulties they had to overcome to be together only intensified their passion. I was born in 1939, almost a year before they married each other.

Cuba was just emerging from the economic crisis of the Depression and the bloody regime of Gerardo Machado. Student revolts, strikes, and protests led, in 1933, to a military coup headed by Sergeant Fulgencio Batista, who became the de facto ruler through a number of presidents who served in name only. But it was a time of renewed possibility, with newly enacted social measures: a minimum wage, eight-hour workday, women's right to vote. Batista was legally elected and served as president from 1940 to 1944. In 1948 he was elected senator, only to organize another bloodless coup, this time against President Carlos Prío Socarrás in 1952, an event that in part led to the Castro revolution.

My father, Carlos Carballo, a.k.a. el Professor Carbell, was an astrologer with a certain notoriety as *adivino*, healer, psychic, and medium, who claimed he could diagnose health problems by reading auras. Whatever it was he did (or perhaps because of his clients' need to believe), he was very successful. He wrote for magazines and newspapers and had a flourishing private practice, a rich source of eccentric characters in itself. My father was a man of many friends and passions, and one of these was food.

Mami too liked exotic foods but she was more of a meat and potatoes kind of cook, which for her meant a rare filet mignon and fried green plantains for breakfast. She couldn't be bothered with the everyday running of the kitchen and relied on Dulce, our cook, for the daily chore of feeding the family. Yet she had a repertoire of unusual (for the forties) dishes she was always happy to prepare for special occasions—a Mexican *pozole*, white gazpacho, and magnificent zabaglione to spoon over a citrus sponge cake, a family favorite.

Our family extended not just to my schizophrenic Aunt Berta, my deaf Uncle Octavio, and my senile but gloriously beautiful grandmother Doña Monona, but also to Tía Patria, the aunt who indulged everyone. The family included my half brothers, my mother's ex-husband, and even his wife and daughters. In addition, there were the family members connected by heart: Pupen, my godmother, Kiki, Pastorita, Ramón, Don Juan and his dog, and many more, all unique in their own way.

Dulce, our cook, was a follower of Santería, a religion that combines Catholic saints and African deities and was first practiced by the African slaves in Cuba. While Dulce let me watch her cook, she would recount the legends of all the deities of Santería, teaching me about their favorite foods and how to stay in their good graces.

Kiki, a gay former aerialist with a country carnival, was my father's general factotum, my mother's confidant and hair colorist. Kiki ironed the fine linens, mended our clothes, sewed on buttons, hemmed my dresses, came early every morning to make the first *café con leche* of the day, and on occasion made chocolate and churros exclusively for me.

Our landlady, Pastorita, was retired from the oldest profession and lived in total seclusion in the downstairs of the once great house we rented. She took it upon herself to teach me how to make the proper *cafecito* and how to light a cigar. Ramón, the numbers runner, came every Saturday morning to take my father's bets and bring us fresh *pastelitos* from the neighborhood bakery. Don Juan, *el carpintero*, who lived in one of Havana's shantytowns, and his dog Joselito were frequent visitors. For Don Juan and Joselito, my dad would drop whatever he was doing to go buy *fritas*, the chorizo and ground beef Cuban answer to the hamburger.

Outside of my home, Havana was an enchanted and enchanting city. Remarkably beautiful, green, luscious, scented, built around a protected bay, its urban rectilinear plan became the blueprint for other colonial cities of the Americas. Squares, fortresses, plazas, promenades, wharves, churches, great houses, palaces, monumental buildings, and miles and miles of columned arcades showed a diversity of styles: Renaissance, Mudéjar Baroque, Neoclassic, Art Deco, Art Nouveau, Cuban Baroque, and innovative twentieth-century construction. The city was magical and its beauty had a heady effect on me. I left briefly to attend Catholic boarding school in the States "to perfect my English and learn some discipline," but I never forgot the city of my heart.

Back in Havana in 1956, for my seventeenth birthday, I surrendered myself to the pervading sensuality of the city and its warmth and rhythm, colors, sounds, smells, and tastes—the indolence that infused our lives. One could physically feel the vibrancy of the city, the *frisson* of danger. In the fifties, even at the height of government corruption, or perhaps because of it, Havana was a nonstop party.

Food and music were at the center of the culture influencing who we were and how we lived. It is hard to believe now, but even as teenagers we frequented the best restaurants and nightclubs. One of our favorites was the improbable Tropicana with its crystal arches and chorus girls who danced on the catwalks among the trees. At all of the clubs, we danced to the music of every great orchestra that played in Havana—Sonora Matancera,

Beny Moré, Fajardo y Sus Estrellas, and any number of others.

But by the late fifties, the political reality of the country loomed over our lives. Fidel Castro had been in the Sierra Maestra since the mid-fifties waging a guerilla war against the Batista government, and by 1957 the revolution had been brought to Havana. Small bombs were being planted in stores, movie houses, and cafés. While they didn't cause major damage, they did cause some injuries and widespread fear. I narrowly escaped two bombings myself.

In the middle of this political turmoil I met Roberto. We dated for about three months, became engaged, and promptly married in December 1958. I was nineteen, he twenty-eight. We had been caught up in the ever-increasing urgency of a society out of control.

In the early morning hours of January 1, 1959, we awoke to the news that Batista had fled the country, providing the de facto triumph of the Revolution. At first we were elated, hoping for a better life out from under Batista's corrupt regime. But soon our joy turned to desperation as new restrictions were put into place hour by hour. Civil liberties were curtailed. All our illusions for a return to democracy were shattered. The slogan of "¿elecciones? ¿para qué?" became the new *cri de guerre*. Fundamental Law was established and in the immediate revolutionary fervor many suspected of being against Fidel or the Revolution were summarily executed.

A few months later the U.S. embargo went into effect and food shortages increased. Out of necessity, my cooking became frugal, limited to the few ingredients available. My father was arrested on trumped up counter revolutionary charges and sentenced to an indefinite number of years in prison. I never saw him again. He died in an psychiatric hospital two years after I left Cuba.

In April 1961, a few days after the Bay of Pigs invasion, Fidel declared Cuba a Communist country. It became clear I had to leave. My husband, Roberto, had no choice but to stay behind. His position as assistant professor at the University of Havana was considered essential to the Revolution and he was not allowed to leave the country.

After much anxiety, many tears, and hurried good-byes, I arrived at the Miami airport on May 20, 1961, with the clothes on my back and no idea when I would ever see my country, my husband, family, or friends again.

It's been over forty years, three-quarters of my life, since I left Havana, but Havana has stayed with me. I have traveled extensively through several continents and earned the Grand Diplôme from Le Cordon Bleu in Paris, and a bachelor's degree in Religious Studies from Fordham University in New York. I also studied regional cuisine in Spain. Certainly these experiences have enriched my life and influenced my cooking, but what defines me as a person are my experiences in Cuba—my family and friends, the "characters" of my childhood, the food and music, the sensual memories of an extraordinary city. These are those stories.

1

HAVANA
IN THE THIRTIES

ONE

Carlos and Sylvia

My father, Carlos Eloy Victor del Carmen Carballo Romero, was born in 1906. He came from a well-to-do family and as the youngest of six children he was very spoiled. There was nothing my grandmother, Abuela Monona, denied him, including a two-seater airplane, a motorcycle, and enough money to support a mistress when he was only seventeen.

When Carlos was around twenty-one, grandfather Don Pancho concluded it was time for him to make some contribution to the family and take his place in society, either as a student or as an apprentice in a relative's plant nursery business. Carlos did not like either choice and besides, he was eager to get away from Havana and the "nice girl" he had promised to marry.

The opportunity for a happy solution came in the form of a traveling carnival that was passing through Havana. He joined "Coney Island Park" as a stunt motorcycle driver. By the time the carnival reached Central America, he had advanced from stunt man to "El Mago de Coney Island Park" and later "el Profesor Carbell"—"Professor" to show deference and respect, a name he continued to use all through his professional life as astrologer, *adivino,* healer, psychic, and medium.

Carlos was a handsome man, very tall for a Cuban. He cut an

imposing figure at six feet, with a fair complexion, black wavy hair, and sea-green eyes. He had the charm and sophistication of George Clooney with the very masculine good looks of Javier Bardem. Women found him irresistible.

Before he returned to Havana in 1936, after his stint with the circus had come to an end, he became quite notorious in San José. Not in a good way. In fact, he had last been seen in Costa Rica in 1932 on the eve of his very public deportation.

After Coney Island Park disbanded, el Profesor Carbell had settled in San José and established a successful practice using his "healing" powers. He came to have an impressive clientele of society ladies and immediately gained a remarkable reputation not only as healer but as seducer as well. The medical establishment saw him as a threat on several fronts and had him arrested for practicing medicine without a license. This, Carbell emphatically denied. His healing techniques, he said, were completely spiritual and involved the mind only, not the body. He did not employ conventional medications, just the use of amulets and charms, and colored waters. Nevertheless he was detained for a few weeks and only released after he had signed several affidavits swearing he would "cease and desist." But naturally he didn't.

After a few months of going about his usual business in a quieter way, he was denounced again. This time no one would intercede for him. A prominent politician's wife was involved and no amount of pleading, public letters, or radio broadcasts in his favor would help.

His alleged threat to medicine and public morals warranted a military detail to escort Profesor Carbell to the coast to board a ship bound for El Salvador. Even the Captain of Police of the city of San José made a special trip to the coast and waited at the docks until he saw the ship carrying my father disappear from view. The *cause célèbre* had now gone beyond being considered a charlatan, or even practicing medicine without a license. It had become a question of honor, as too many society ladies had become his "patients."

The interim years of 1932 to 1936, when he returned to Havana, remain a complete mystery, though I imagine he continued his adventures and his same practices in other Latin American countries.

By the time my father returned to Cuba he was said to be an experienced astrologer, and my grandmother (forever indulging him) allowed the prodigal son to establish his *consultorio* in her home. He read auras to diagnose illness, brought messages from the beyond, and in spite of conventional wisdom, he proved himself a healer. His practice included politicians, actors, and many, many ladies. He was a very powerful psychic and used astrology as one of his tools. Carlos again had become an immediate success and soon established a clientele just as impressive as the one in San José.

Sylvia

My mom, Sylvia Molé Betancourt, born in 1910, also came from a large family, but most of her brothers and sisters were half brothers and sisters, eleven or twelve in total, possibly more; a most unusual occurrence in the early twentieth century in Cuba or anyplace else for that matter. But much was unusual about her family.

My grandmother América left her first husband and four children to run away to Costa Rica with my mother's father. It was scandalous, especially since it didn't last long. They separated after two or three years, but bravely, especially for my grandmother, returned to their small town of Manzanillo in Oriente province to go their separate ways. Molé went on to form three other unions and have several more children. América went back to live with her mother and the children she had previously abandoned.

My mother grew up in reduced circumstances—there was absolutely no money left, everything had been sold: land, cattle, properties, all going to support the independence wars against Spain. The sacrifices were worth it. Cuba became independent and a cousin of my great-grandmother became the first president of the Republic, and another the first rector of the University of Havana. We are still very proud of that.

For my mother there was also embarrassment, not shame—my grandmother was too proud for shame—but growing up without a father present in a small town was difficult. However, it was an enriching environment. My mother's home was a spirited household; my Abuela América and my great-grandmother Doña Gertrudis played the piano and the guitar respectively and sat in the open parlor every afternoon serenading the passersby. Their house was the meeting point for the extended family, including my mother's half siblings on her father's side and many friends. Abuela América was also a poet and a free spirit. Her intellectual friends, artists, writers, poets—all men—came to her weekly salon for music, poetry readings, pastries, coffee, and cigars.

Abuela América further complicated the family dynamics by dying at age fifty-two, leaving my mother at thirteen unprotected by her father and in the hands of my mother's eldest half sister (on her mother's side), the twenty-three-year-old, energetic Tía Patria. Tía looked after Sylvia until she was seventeen when she thought it was time for Sylvia to marry.

Tía Patria wanted only the best for Mami and thought it was time for Sylvia to have some stability in her life. Mami thought herself too young, too battered, too fragile, simply not ready to assume the responsibilities of a husband, children, a household. But Tía insisted, and through friends of the family she introduced her to Aubrey, a handsome British engineer freshly arrived from

Kingston, Jamaica. Aubrey, born and educated in London, had quickly fallen in love with the tropics and just as promptly fell in love with Sylvia. He made an excellent candidate for marriage. But there was a problem.

Sylvia had only gone to school as far as the third grade. She had come home crying one day because a nun had called her a heathen and a bastard and had made her kneel on corn kernels in a corner of the classroom as atonement for her mother's sins. Abuela América made the instant decision not to send her back to school and teach her at home herself. But Sylvia had only been nine at the time of the incident and from then on her learning had been erratic. She read whatever she wanted, as Abuela América never followed much of a syllabus. Without proper schooling, and overprotected at home, Sylvia had remained a bit of a wild child. At seventeen, she was still swimming in the river and climbing trees with the boys, marriage the last thing on her mind.

Aubrey was a gentle, sincere man and wanted Sylvia to make an informed decision before accepting his proposal. He wanted to polish her a little and show her a world other than the interior patio of her home. He offered to send Sylvia to his mother, who was now living in Kingston, where she could go to school, or even to London for finishing school. But Tía Patria roundly refused on the grounds that a young woman could not accept a gift of that magnitude without compromising herself and dishonoring the family. There had been plenty of that in the past, thank you. But Aubrey, in spite of his well-founded apprehensions, soon married Sylvia, who was more than reluctant to commit.

Braised Chicken

When friends dropped by to visit my grandmother and great-grandmother, they often brought fowl they had hunted or raised, fish they had caught, and the occasional piglet. No invitations were necessary—everyone who was around stayed for dinner. In Manzanillo, in the early 1900s, they made this dish with guinea fowl *(pintada)* and in the fifties Mami always made it as part of our Christmas Eve dinner. Now guinea hens are difficult to find, often only available as a special order during Thanksgiving and Christmas, so I have substituted a large chicken. The dish doesn't have the same depth of taste as when made with *pintada,* but it is very good anyway.

One 4- to 5-pound chicken
1 teaspoon salt
½ teaspoon freshly ground black pepper
1 teaspoon saffron threads
1 teaspoon coriander seeds
½ teaspoon cumin seed
4 tablespoons olive oil
1 medium onion, diced
3 garlic cloves, pressed or minced
Zest (in one piece) and juice of 1 lemon
1 cup chicken broth
1 bay leaf
2 egg yolks
2 tablespoons minced parsley

Rinse the chicken, dry with paper towels, and place in a bowl.

Pulverize the spices in a spice grinder or mini food processor or with a mortar and pestle. Add 2 tablespoons of the olive oil to make a paste. Prick the chicken deeply with a fork and rub with the paste inside and out. Cover and allow to marinate about 4 hours: 3 hours in the fridge and 1 hour on the kitchen counter to bring to room temperature.

Heat the remaining 2 tablespoons olive oil in a Dutch oven or heavy pan over medium-high heat. Brown the chicken well, about 2 minutes on each side. Add the onion and sauté until it colors. Add the garlic and stir. Add the lemon zest and juice, chicken broth, and bay leaf. Set the chicken with the breast up. Cover and cook over low heat for about 1 hour and 30 minutes, or a little longer, turning every 30 minutes. It is supposed to be well done and very tender.

Remove the bay leaf and lemon zest from the pan and discard. Place the chicken on a serving platter and keep warm. Remove as much fat as possible from the cooking juices and keep them simmering on the stove.

In a bowl, whisk the egg yolks well. Add a little of the hot cooking juices to the yolks and whisk vigorously. Pour the yolks into the cooking juices and whisk until thickened to the consistency of cream, making sure the sauce doesn't curdle. (If it does, give it a few whizzes in a food processor or blender. It won't be the best, but it is not the end of the world either.)

Spoon the sauce over the chicken and serve.

TWO

Thunderbolts in Eden

My parents met at the Jardín Botánico, the University of Havana's plant research facility, an idyllic garden full of exotic plants and flowers, greenhouses, and plenty of space for children to play. Every morning Sylvia took her two little boys, Clive and Aubrey, there. Carlos lived nearby and often took his morning walk on the grounds.

One of those mornings, Carlos approached her, looking straight into her eyes with his otherwordly look. He had been watching her for some time and it was several days before he approached her. He was holding four cones of melting *granizado*—yellow, red, green, and blue—in his hands as they were an afterthought. The boys smiled. Sylvia had no alternative but to take the ices from him before they melted completely.

At the time my parents met, in the mid thirties, Cuba was just emerging from the economic crisis of the Great Depression and the political upheaval of Gerardo Machado's regime. Student revolts, strikes, and protests had led to a military coup headed by Sergeant Fulgencio Batista. Batista claimed he did not want to be president and installed a temporary government (he was the power behind the throne) with the promise of free democratic elections. It was a time of renewed possibility.

My dad was freshly arrived from his long sojourn in Central America, and Sylvia was trapped in a loveless marriage to a British engineer. They could have not been more different; he was the urban sophisticate, she the inexperienced housewife recently moved to Havana.

My mother later described their meeting as being caught at sea *en una galerna,* the northwest wind that strikes the Cantabric coast with catastrophic waves. She had no more control of herself than she would have of a small craft in a deadly storm. My father, more of a fantasist, described their meeting as a sortilege. She had quite simply bewitched him. Neither her married status nor his recent nuptials to the "nice girl" (the same girl he had left behind to join the traveling carnival) seemed to interfere with their immediate reality.

Sylvia's history of loneliness and longing brought her close to Carlos very quickly. She was twenty-six, Carlos twenty-nine. They only married after my birth in 1939, three years after they first met. They went to Mexico on their honeymoon, and Mami always observed their anniversary with *pozole,* a dish they had shared at the Mercado Central. Dessert was watermelon ice.

Pozole

Pozole is a dish perfect for sharing. Everyone is served communally, and the garnishes, essential to round off the flavors, are passed around the table. Usually made with pork, it is a popular dish in Mexico and many versions exist. This lighter recipe, made with chicken, was given to me by a cousin who has lived in Mexico City for the last thirty-five years.

For the Pozole

5 ancho chiles,* soaked in warm water until soft
4 pounds chicken legs and thighs, cut into halves
One 2-inch-long cinnamon stick
1 whole head garlic (unpeeled)
1 large onion (peeled)
1 teaspoon salt
*Two 15½-ounce cans (3 cups) hominy, rinsed in water and well
   drained*

For the Hot Sauce

10 jalapeño chiles, deveined and seeded
½ cup white vinegar
½ teaspoon salt

For the Garnishes

1 head red leaf lettuce, cut in chiffonade
8 radishes, very thinly sliced
1 onion, minced
4 Key limes, cut in wedges
2 tablespoons dried oregano

1 small avocado, diced (optional)

**Ancho chiles are dried poblanos, which add a smoky taste and
depth of flavor.*

To make the *pozole,* discard the ancho chile veins and seeds and
process the chiles in a food processor to make a thin puree. Place
the chicken in a heavy casserole with the cinnamon stick, head of
garlic, onion, salt, and chile puree and cover with 3 quarts water,
or more if necessary. Bring to a boil and then lower the heat to a
simmer. Cover the pot, leaving a small opening for the steam to
escape. Cook for about 1 hour, until the chicken is fall-off-the-
bones tender. Discard the garlic, onion, and cinnamon stick.

Add the rinsed hominy and cook for an additional 10 minutes.

While the chicken cooks, prepare the hot sauce and garnishes.
To make the sauce, puree the jalapeños, vinegar, and salt in a
food processor or blender until smooth. Transfer to a bowl and
allow to rest at room temperature.

Set the garnishes in small bowls on the table. Set the *pozole* pot
in the center. Serve the *pozole* and pass the condiments to add to
taste to each individual serving. Accompany with corn tortillas
sautéed in oil.

Watermelon Ice

One of our childhood pleasures was fruit-flavored, brightly colored ices. No one could pretend they were healthy—they were
just refreshing and delicious in the heat. These beauties came in a
two-wheel pushcart made heavy by a very large block of ice. On
the sides of the cart were tall bottles filled with very sweet colored syrups. You chose your flavor and the "operator" shaved the
ice, scooped it into a paper cone, and poured the syrup on top.
You got a straw and after the first sip—straight to heaven. This
version is all fruit, no syrup, the way Mami made it at home.

3 pounds ripe watermelon
½ cup sugar

Scoop out the pulp of the watermelon into a bowl and carefully
seed. Break into chunks. Process the melon together with the
sugar in a food processor or blender. Transfer to an ice cream
maker and follow the manufacturer's instructions. Or place in a
shallow container in the freezer. Every 20 minutes, scrape with a
fork, making sure to reach the crystals formed around the edges.
Do this for 2 hours or until the ice is frozen. Before serving, place
in the refrigerator for about 15 minutes to soften slightly.

2

HAVANA
IN THE FORTIES

THREE

Havana Through My Father's Eyes

My father was devoted to his clients. Granted, he made them wait to see him, but once he was with someone, that person held his complete attention; everything else faded away. He would hold eye contact with such fierce intensity the person felt a profound connection to him, what he would call a "soul connection." Equally powerful were the amulets he made for his clients that were meant to protect them from bad luck and evil spirits. I clearly remember donating my nail clippings and strands of hair to the enterprise. Papi maintained that any part of a pure being (meaning me) gave special strength to the amulet.

Papi's "business" was very successful, and he must have been good at it. Part healer, part medium, part astrologer, and complete irresistible charmer, it was how he earned a living. While we were not in the summer-in-Europe category, I did go to private school, we had our little cottage on the beach, and he drove a Mercury Coupe—a present from a grateful client. These were prosperous times and the standard of living was high.

Apart from his professional life, his private life was filled with fantasy. My dad was an inveterate treasure hunter. He had dived hard hat off the coast of Pinar del Río on the trail of a Spanish galleons sunk near the shore. Doubloons awaited. He had the maps to prove it. We would be rich beyond our dreams.

He had dozens of get-rich-quick schemes. One was the cure for cancer; the secret was in the seeds of peaches. He planted some trees on land that belonged to Abuelo Don Pancho, but his attention turned to beehives before the trees gave fruit. The royal jelly followed, which was not only good for just about any illness but used in beauty creams as well. Surely you could make money with that. The Jesuits owed our family hundreds of millions of dollars, was how I heard him tell the story. One of his great-grandfathers (or some other equally distant relative) had made the Jesuits a substantial loan to build schools in Cuba, and not only was there a large principal, but imagine the interest that had accrued. He was going to sue them; we would be rich.

For all of his scheming, Papi was a man of many friends and passions, and one of these was food. He would crisscross Havana, stopping at every kiosk and counter, sampling whatever was being offered. He talked to everyone and *contaba cuentos,* told stories. It was thrilling to go with him and be part of the stories, the food, and the sights of the city.

We took long drives along the Malecón. We drove along the narrow streets of La Habana Vieja, the old part of the city, where I liked to pretend that if I stretched my arms out, I could touch the houses on both sides of the street at the same time. My favorite tour was along El Paséo del Prado, the majestic tree-lined boulevard built in 1772 and one of the first structures to be built outside the city walls. There were scattered plaques on the houses that faced the boulevard commemorating some historical point of interest, like the one at number 156 Prado, where in 1881 the Cuban physician Carlos Finlay first expounded his theory about mosquitoes being the carriers of yellow fever. One of our obligations was to stop in front of the house to pay our respects. While Papi saluted, I had to make a little curtsy. It was one of our many rituals.

Part of the pleasure of going out with my father was that everyone seemed to know him and even if people didn't stop to talk to him, they would wave and smile. The boulevard was a popular place for pedestrians. The lively streets around it burst with dozens of cafeterias, cafés, bakeries, peanut vendors, orange sellers, ices, and *ostiones*. My dad loved every kind of food and always encouraged me to sample right along with him. He took pleasure in every bite. It was a joyful experience, and since then I have always associated food with being cosseted, with being happy.

We searched for the perfect *frita* stand (Cuba's version of hamburger) in each neighborhood, even though we favored Sebastián's, located on the corner of Zapata and Paséo. For stuffed potatoes we had to go across the bay to Guanabacóa; sandwiches, Cuban sandwiches, of course, were best made by Paco at 10th and 23rd. We visited the central market and often had a lunch of lobster with mayonnaise in a nearby *bodegón*. But we favored kiosks and stands rather than established eateries, the more modest the better.

Our all-time-favorite food indulgence was the *bar de ostiones*, an ambitious name for a small kiosk on wheels. The *ostiones*, a type of mollusk that grows in mangroves and tastes like oysters, were kept fresh in small narrow glasses embedded right into a block of ice. We had a favorite kiosk too, the one parked at the corner of San Lázaro and Infanta, but sometimes we'd drive around until we found another one that suited us better. Our standards of selection depended on our mood that day: a big block of ice meant the seller had just set up, a long line of people meant either he had fresh product or that he was a joker in that special Cuban way of making fun of everything. When we settled on a particular kiosk, Papi would stop in the middle of traffic, make a feeble attempt to park by creating a space where there was none, and we'd both get out of the car.

We liked our *ostiones* with a generous squirt of lemon juice. The trick was to knock them back all at once and hold them in your mouth for a few seconds before swallowing to get every single briny molecule you had coming to you. They tasted like the sea. After each happy shot, Papi and I would smile, toast each other with the empty glass, nodding our heads in agreement to have another. I knew there were few children who liked raw oysters and fewer still who had special moments like this with their fathers.

Invariably our last stop before going home was at the best Chinese fruit and vegetable stand on Galiano street, where we bought fruit for my mother so she wouldn't feel completely left out.

Papi also introduced me to Middle Eastern food through Turkish friends who, lacking a proper restaurant, served food in their dining room. (An idea that under the revolutionary government became popular as *paladares.*) There I had *kofte,* thick yogurt, and salads spiked with fresh mint for the first time, as well as nut-filled cookies that have remained fresh in my taste memory to this day.

On Sundays, when Dulce, our spirited cook, had her day off, my parents, my brother Aubrey, and I would often go to Rancho Luna, a popular grill just outside Havana. Our older brother, Clive, was living with his father and thought himself too sophisticated for our family outings. The restaurant itself consisted of a wide porch all around the central structure (no one ever sat indoors), and the roof was thatched with palm fronds, like the *campesino* houses. Chicken over a wood grill was *la especialidad de la casa,* the home-grown, corn-fed chickens seasoned with a delicious marinade that has remained secret to this day (see page 30).

Or Papi would take us to El Pacífico, a Chinatown restaurant, to visit another friend of his, Andrés Wong, a Cuban Chinese waiter. Much to our delight, Andrés would bring out dish upon dish that appeared nowhere in the menu, oyster pancakes, pork rib tea soup, bon-bon chicken salad, which I liked to order because I thought it came with chocolates. Especially for my father, Andrés always asked one of the cooks to make roast duck with a soy sauce and honey lacquer. My favorite dish was *maripositas fritas,* fried butterflies. It was only many years later, long after the magic had gone, that I learned to call them fried wontons.

Roast Duck El Pacífico

El Pacífico was the best restaurant in Chinatown and quite an institution. It occupied the fifth floor and terrace of a narrow building at the corner of Cuchillo and San Nicolás, the very heart of Havana's Chinatown. Going up the rickety elevator with room for five, including the operator, you went past several gambling parlors and Chinese societies, which often played strident Cantonese music. Of course, that was part of the charm and the authenticity of the place. This recipe is a reconstruction of the flavors as I remember them.

One 4- to 5-pound duck
Salt and freshly ground black pepper to taste
1 tablespoon canola oil
⅓ cup chopped onion
⅓ cup chopped celery
⅓ cup chopped fresh ginger
2 garlic cloves, pressed or minced
1 cinnamon stick, broken
1 star anise
¼ cup soy sauce
¼ cup honey
3 tablespoons Chinese or balsamic vinegar
Watercress for garnish

In a large pasta pot bring about 10 cups water to a boil, lower the duck to scald for about 4 to 5 minutes and remove quickly. Drain the duck and discard the water.

Dry the duck with paper towels inside and out and place in a large bowl. Refrigerate overnight without covering to make a crisper skin.

When ready to cook, preheat the oven to 450°F. Salt and pepper the duck inside and out.

Heat the oil in a skillet and sauté the onion, celery, and ginger until soft. Add the garlic, cinnamon, star anise, and 1 teaspoon of the soy sauce. Stir to mix well and rub all over, including into the cavity leaving the remaining flavorings inside. Close the cavity by sewing or lacing with small metal skewers and string. Combine the remaining soy sauce, honey, and vinegar and set aside. Place the duck on a baking rack over a drip pan containing several inches of water to reduce smoking. Roast for 30 minutes at 450°F. Reduce the oven temperature to 250°F and roast for 30 minutes. Remove the duck from the oven and discard all water and fat. Pour the soy sauce, honey, and vinegar mixture over the duck and return to the oven for another 30 minutes, basting at least once. Remove the duck to a cutting board and cut into serving pieces. Place on a warm platter and pour the cooking juices over it. Garnish with watercress.

Wontons

I prefer the homemade version of these little jewels and have been changing the recipe over the years, as there are so many versions. I like to serve them with a sweet and sour sauce, and with a stunningly hot Chinese mustard as well.

For the Dipping Sauce

¾ cup bitter-orange marmalade

3 tablespoons sweet soy sauce

2 tablespoons white vinegar

For the Wontons

½ pound finely minced pork

½ pound minced shrimp

½ cup finely shredded bok choy

½ cup chopped bean sprouts

5 chives, minced

2 garlic cloves, smashed

1 tablespoon grated fresh ginger

1 teaspoon dark brown sugar

1 tablespoon soy sauce

2 tablespoons vegetable oil

2 tablespoons cornstarch

Salt and freshly ground black pepper to taste

2 tablespoons rice or white vinegar

30 wonton wrappers

Canola oil for frying

Hot Chinese mustard for serving

To make the dipping sauce, heat the marmalade in a small pot, stirring to dissolve. Add the soy sauce and vinegar, stir, and set aside.

For the wontons, combine the pork, shrimp, vegetables, garlic, and ginger with the brown sugar and soy sauce in a bowl. Heat the oil in a large skillet and sauté the mixture until the pork is no longer pink, the vegetables are soft, and the liquid has mostly evaporated. Add salt and pepper. Stir the cornstarch into the vinegar to dissolve and add to the skillet. Stir for about 2 minutes or until slightly thickened and glazed. Drain any excess liquid and refrigerate until completely cool.

Place about 1 teaspoon of the wonton mixture just off center on a wonton wrapper. Moisten the edges with water and fold corner to corner to make a triangle. Press the edges firmly. Pull the corners around the filling behind the folded edge as if you were making fortune cookie. Moisten your fingers and press the bottom of one point against the top of the other.

Cover with a moistened towel until all the wontons are made.

Heat about 1 inch oil in a cast iron Dutch oven or heavy pot and fry at medium-high heat, about 375°F, adding one at a time so they don't stick. Swirl the oil with the back of a slotted spoon and fry until golden on all sides, about 2 to 3 minutes. Drain on paper towels and keep warm in a 200°F oven until ready to serve with the dipping sauce.

Poached Lobster with
Homemade Lobster Mayonnaise

One of my favorite places to go with my dad was La Plaza del Vapor near the docks, one of the several huge central markets in Havana. My mom thought it was too crowded and too dirty for me and she didn't like my going, so it was bound to be my favorite of favorites partly because it was forbidden, partly because of the many merchants who knew Papi, but mostly, because we always ended up for lunch at the *bodegón* across the street.

We would sit at the bar and watch the *bodeguero* prepare the mayonnaise in a large, well-cured mortar and pestle where he vigorously stirred egg yolks and olive oil, adding salt and lemon juice until he got the optimum smooth texture. Then, and only then, would he plunge the freshly caught lobsters in a large pot of boiling seawater for the just the perfect amount of time.

This is one of the taste memories that is seared in my mind and why lobster always brings back thoughts of my father.

For the Lobster

Three 2-pound female spiny lobsters
2 tablespoons sea salt
A handful of fresh seaweed (if available)

For the Mayonesa de Langosta

2 egg yolks
Salt and freshly ground black pepper to taste
3 tablespoons freshly squeezed lemon juice, or more to taste
Lobsters' tomalley (green) and eggs (very dark red) if available
1½ cups extra virgin olive oil or a combination of olive oil and a
    neutral-flavored oil for a milder taste

Fill a stock pot three-quarters full of room temperature water, add salt and seaweed if available, then slip the lobsters into the poaching liquid. As soon as the water starts to simmer, start counting the time, 30 to 35 minutes, or until the lobster reaches an internal temperature of 160°F with an instant-read thermometer. Cooking the lobster slowly allows the meat to be more tender.

Twist the lobsters' heads over a bowl to collect all the juices. Collect the tomalley (the green stuff) and eggs, if lucky enough to get them, and reserve separately. Press each lobster on its side— there will be a small crunch. Using both hands, pull the sides of the lobsters apart. The shell should break and the meat will pop out.

Using a sharp knife, cut into ½-inch medallions and place in the bowl where you have collected the juices. Let cool at room temperature until the mayonnaise is made.

Place the egg yolks, salt, and lemon juice in a food processor or blender along with ¼ cup of the oil and blend. When well blended, start adding the rest of the oil in a slow steady stream.

Once you have added about half the oil and the mixture thickens, add the tomalley and eggs. With the machine still running, add the rest of the oil a little faster. Taste, and if necessary adjust the seasoning with more salt, a little pepper, and lemon juice. If the mayonnaise seems too thick, add a little hot water, or in this case the juices of the lobsters.

To make a simple mayonnaise proceed the same way but leave out the tomalley and lobster eggs. To make aïoli (garlic mayonnaise), add 2 to 4 pressed or minced garlic cloves when you first begin to blend. For more depth of taste, roast the garlic.

Pollo Rancho Luna (Chicken with Adobo)

In the Havana of the fifties there was a very popular country restaurant called Rancho Luna. It had been built to resemble an old hacienda house and it had a wide veranda all around. With its land and fruit trees it became a perfect place for families to while away the best part of a Sunday. Kids ran around freely, climbing trees and having a good time while parents leisurely enjoyed the specialty of the house—a grilled chicken marinated in a secret family adobo recipe. I've developed a version with a good approximation to the original taste, or so I think. I also butterfly and flatten the chicken even if Rancho Luna did not, just because.

For the Adobo

2 tablespoons olive oil
1 teaspoon salt
Freshly ground black pepper to taste
2 garlic cloves, pressed or minced
1 teaspoon lime juice

For the Chicken

One 3½- to 3¾-pound chicken
2 tablespoons olive oil

To Finish

¾ cup minced onion
½ cup minced parsley
Juice of 2 Key limes

Combine all the adobo ingredients in an 8-inch square glass pan and reserve.

To butterfly the chicken, place breast side down. Using heavy-duty kitchen shears, cut along both sides of the backbone. Discard the backbone, turn the chicken over with the breast facing you, and give it a good whack to break the breastbone and flatten.

Place the chicken in the adobo, turn several times to coat well, and cover. Leave at room temperature for about an hour, turning once, or refrigerate overnight.

When ready to cook, preheat the oven to 500°F. Heat the olive oil in a cast iron Dutch oven or skillet over high heat. Lightly pat the chicken with paper towels.

Place the chicken skin side down in the pan and cook for 3 to 5 minutes on the stove until well browned. Careful, it splatters! Remove from the heat and turn the chicken breast up.

Turn the oven down to 400°F. Place the chicken in the oven and bake for about 40 minutes, always maintaining the high temperature. Baste twice and continue cooking until the chicken is no longer pink and an instant-read thermometer registers 185°F. Remove the chicken to a serving platter and cover loosely with aluminum foil.

Place the pan on the stove and add the onion, parsley, and lime juice. Swirl around, scraping up the brown bits at the bottom of the pan, and pour over the gorgeously browned EAT-ME-NOW chicken.

Pistachio Cookies

When Papi took me to have lunch with the Turkish family, we always had these cookies for dessert, Papi with his *cafecito*, I with homemade pistachio ice cream.

> *½ cup pistachios*
> *½ cup dried cranberries, chopped by hand*
> *1 egg*
> *1 egg yolk*
> *¾ cup sugar*
> *1 tablespoon flour*
> *6 egg whites*

Place a silicone baking mat on the baking sheet or lightly brush the pan with butter. Preheat the oven to 275°F. Pulse the pistachios coarsely in a food processor so as not to overprocess. Place the pistachios in a large bowl, add the cranberries, and mix.

Cream the whole egg and the yolk with ½ cup of the sugar until fluffy and pale. Add to the nut and cranberry mixture. Add the flour, and stir to mix well.

Beat the egg whites to soft peaks while gradually adding the remaining sugar. Gently fold into the nut mixture.

Scoop up a rounded teaspoon of the batter and use another spoon to push the batter onto the prepared baking sheet, allowing 2 inches between each cookie for spreading. Bake for 25 to 30 minutes, until springy-firm and lightly browned. Makes 3 dozen.

FOUR

Mami
and Life at Home

Unconventional in everything from mothering skills to the way she ate, Mami nevertheless doted on my brothers and me, indulging us even if supervising at a distance from a comfortable chair where she sat to read a good portion of the day.

Mami deplored ugliness and fortunately for us we were three handsome kids. Her relationship with my brother Clive was special. He was the smartest one and they seemed to have a very strong connection, he being the first born. Aubrey made her laugh with all his pranks and innocent mischief. She defended and protected him, claiming he needed more attention than either Clive or me since in the scheme of things he was the middle child. With me, the relationship was a little different. I was the youngest, the only girl, and the only child of my father's, so I was very, very spoiled. Still, the story goes that when I was a newborn, I did not like her to hold me. I cried, arched my back, and fussed until she put me down or gave me to someone else to hold. She was a very good mother even though I always perceived her as a little distant. In truth she was very affectionate with all three of us; we got hugs and kisses and we sat on her lap a lot. I remember her playing with me and having tea with my dolls, but my principal maternal relationship was always with my Pupen, my godmother. Ours was an eccentric and very animated household. There were numerous comings and goings from a cast of characters we called family and friends. My schizophrenic Tía Berta shared a room with my senile Abuela Monona. Tío Octavio, who was profoundly deaf, was absent during the day working or visiting his fiancée of twenty years at night, but always coming home to sleep. Ramón, the numbers runner, Kiki, former aerialist and general factotum of the household, Don Juan the carpenter and his little dog Joselito were constant visitors. A rare tropical turtle lived unhappily in the bathtub, displaced every time someone took a shower. Pupen, my godmother, also lived with us and Dulce, the cook, arrived early every morning encased in her fierce warrior attitude. Aunts and cousins came often and there were ten things going on at once. *Café* was made fresh for every visitor. And of course, there was my father's waiting room in the front parlor, overflowing with clients, and his draped *consultorio* in the smaller parlor.

There always was a considerable amount of cooking going on, enough food to welcome the many regular and unexpected guests who were served any time they arrived, regardless of the time of day. The only ones who ate on a schedule were the kids.

My mom and dad ate dinner together whenever my father took a break from his practice, but until nine-thirty or ten, people streamed in and out and ate as they came and went. It was sturdy fare—oxtail stew, pork chops, and always rice and beans and plantains or another tropical tuber. For herself and Papi, Mami (not Dulce) prepared seafood dishes, like her *camarones a la crema,* shrimp in a cream sauce, which Papi was crazy about.

Often, rather late, when Papi had finished his last consultation, he and Mami dressed up and went dancing and gambling into the Havana night. Frequently their return home coincided with my waking up. I loved it when Mami prepared my breakfast while still wearing her evening clothes. She would sometimes bring me *filloas,* a Galician specialty, from one of the popular Spanish restaurants of the era and sprinkle these large crepes with sugar while the milk boiled for my *café con leche.* She, herself, favored filet mignon and *tostones* for her own breakfast.

Mornings, while Papi slept for a few hours, Mami tried to organize the chaos. Afternoons, while my father saw to his clients, she read and rested and mostly brooded. My mom and dad were passionately in love with each other, but my father was unable to be faithful, and Mami would often receive anonymous letters and phone calls with details of his indiscretions.

I was still a small child and she in her early thirties when she developed pain in her joints for which a dear friend of the family, Dr. Carlos Pitaluga, noted physician and refugee from Franco's Spain, prescribed a blank check and a life away from my father. We thought it was funny.

Camarones a la Crema
(Shrimp in Cream Sauce)

This is one of the dishes Mami prepared herself. Plain white rice and *tostones* go great with this dish.

2 tablespoons unsalted butter
1 pound medium shrimp, cleaned and rinsed
4 garlic cloves, minced
½ teaspoon salt
½ cup finely chopped parsley
⅓ cup warm heavy cream

In a heavy skillet heat the butter at high heat until it stops bubbling, but don't let it brown. Add the shrimp and stir vigorously until they begin to color. Add the garlic, continue to stir, then add the salt and parsley and stir. Add the cream and bring to a quick boil. The shrimp should not cook more than about 4 minutes total. Serve at once.

Rabo Encendido (Oxtail Stew)

This is one of the few dishes in Cuban cooking that is spicy hot, and I like to make it with a heavy dose of Spanish *pimentón picante*, a type of spicy paprika. Serve with white rice and slightly caramelized fried ripe plantains.

4 to 5 pounds oxtail, cut in pieces
About 1 cup flour
2 teaspoons salt
½ teaspoon freshly ground black pepper
2 tablespoons pimentón
¼ cup olive oil, or more if needed
1 large onion, chopped
5 garlic cloves, sliced
1 green bell pepper, seeded and chopped
2 large tomatoes, seeded and grated
1 tablespoon fresh thyme
1 tablespoon fresh oregano
2 to 3 sprigs fresh rosemary
2 bay leaves
2 cups red wine
About 1 cup beef broth

Rinse the oxtails and pat dry. Combine the flour, salt, pepper, and pimentón. Dredge the oxtail pieces in this mixture. Pat to remove excess flour.

Heat the olive oil in a Dutch oven or heavy casserole and brown the meat at medium-high heat without scorching. Remove to a plate.

Add a little more oil if needed, then add the onion, garlic, and bell pepper. Cook for about 3 minutes at medium heat, then add the grated tomato and stir. Continue cooking until the vegetables have wilted.

Return the browned oxtails to the pot and add the herbs and red wine. Add enough broth to reach the top of the meat but don't cover it. Bring to a boil, reduce the heat to a simmer, and cover. Cook for 2 hours and 30 minutes or until the meat falls off the bones. Remove the meat to a deep serving platter and keep warm. Reduce the sauce at high heat for 3 or 4 minutes. Taste the sauce, adjust the seasoning, pour over the meat, and serve.

Fricasé de Pollo (Chicken Stew)

This is another typical who-knew-how-many-people-it-had-to-feed, able-to-wait-on-the-stove-until-called-upon-dish, easy to make with common ingredients. It is fabulous as leftovers.

For the last forty-five years, give or take a few, I've been tinkering with this recipe and changing it as my palate changed. I now like to make it with dark meat, red pepper flakes or hot *pimentón*, and grated lemon zest and parsley for a fresh burst of flavor.

3 to 4 pounds dark chicken meat, cut in chunks
1 teaspoon salt
Freshly ground black pepper to taste
2 tablespoons olive oil, or more if needed
1 cup chopped onion
5 garlic cloves, minced
1 ripe tomato, grated
1 teaspoon tomato paste
Red pepper flakes or hot pimentón to taste
½ cup golden raisins
⅓ cup olives, pitted and sliced
½ cup jarred roasted red peppers, sliced
¼ cup capers
¼ cup sliced pitted green olives
½ cup chicken broth or white wine
Grated zest of 1 lemon mixed with ½ cup minced parsley

Wash and dry the chicken pieces and remove all visible fat. Salt and pepper generously.

In a deep, heavy skillet or Dutch oven heat the olive oil and lightly brown the chicken pieces in two batches to avoid overcrowding. (Overcrowding causes steam and prevents meat from browning properly.)

Remove the chicken pieces from the skillet and keep warm. Add 1 more tablespoon oil if necessary. Sauté the onion until wilted while scraping the pan with a wooden spoon. Add the rest of the ingredients except for the lemon zest and parsley. Stir.

Return the chicken to the casserole and stir to coat the chicken pieces. Cover, turn the heat down to a simmer, and cook for about 40 minutes. Transfer the chicken pieces to a serving platter. Add the lemon zest–parsley combination to the pot, stir, and pour cooking juices over the chicken.

Tostones
(Fried Green Plantains)

Everyone is familiar with *tostones* and while they are really simple to make it is easier to learn how to make them if someone shows you. They have to be fried twice, like the best French fries, and the oil temperature, as well as the texture (or doneness) of the plantain slices after the first frying, is important. The firmness of the blow (to flatten them) determines the thickness.

Vegetable oil for frying
2 large green plantains
Salt to taste

Fill a large skillet a third full with oil and heat to medium-low (325°F).

Peel the plantains and cut into 1-inch slices. Deep-fry the plantain slices for 3 to 4 minutes, just until they begin to color very lightly. Turn and cook on the other side. Do not overcrowd the skillet. Drain on paper towels.

When slightly cooled, place a piece of brown paper bag or paper towel on top of each slice and, using your fist, flatten to about ¼ inch thick. Do this while they're hot, as otherwise they will harden as they cool.

After flattening the plantain slices, you can hold until ready to fry a second time.

Heat the oil to 375°F and return the plantain slices to the skillet. Fry for another 2 to 3 minutes until golden and crispy, turning once. You can tell when they are done because they make a hollow sound when flicked.

Drain over paper towels again, sprinkle with salt, and serve hot. At home we thought *tostones* went with everything and they were available practically at every meal.

Filloas

Known as *filloas* in Galicia and *frixuelos* in Asturias, these large crepes can be eaten rolled with sprinkled sugar, any kind of jam, whipped cream, or pastry cream. Using broth in the batter makes the crepes lighter and deepens their flavor.

2 large eggs, slightly beaten
¾ cup chicken broth
¾ cup whole milk
1 teaspoon sugar
Pinch of salt
2 cups sifted flour, more or less
About 4 tablespoons melted sweet butter

In a large bowl, beat together the eggs, broth, milk, sugar, and salt. When well mixed, start adding the flour little by little until it becomes a smooth, loose batter. Cover and allow to rest for 1 hour.

The *filloas* are best made in an 8- or 9-inch nonstick skillet. Brush a little melted butter on the pan. Using a ladle or measuring cup, pour a small amount of batter in the center of the pan, just enough to coat the pan when swirled. As soon as the *filloa* is set, turn and cook briefly on the other side. Be sure not to brown. Keep warm until the whole batch is made. Roll with your favorite filling. Eat warm.

FIVE

The Cook

My mother cooked occasionally, a special dish or a special request, and she set the menus. But in the kitchen, Dulce was queen.

Dulce was a very light-skinned *mulata* with blondish hair. She had a rather large bosom (where she kept the house keys) and was known to use it as a weapon. When she was mad at my dad, which was often, she would get very close to him and give him such a whack with her boobs that he would lose his balance.

Dulce liked to say that she was tall for her height and young for her age. I don't think she was much taller than five feet and she must have been in her early thirties, but to me, she seemed a giant and very old. She wasn't fat, but hefty and compact. She never moved without purpose and never talked unless she had something to say. No one would have considered her pretty, yet she did have an allure—her stillness made her attractive. And she was feisty. Her signals were very clear: "Do *not* mess with me."

Dulce had a lot of style and wore a blue kerchief around her neck in a certain way, which she called *"al desprecio,"* with disdain. She wouldn't be caught dead without the necklaces of blue and white beads she always wore to assure the protection of her patron saint, Yemayá. Her attitude was that she did not, would not, try all that hard to make herself beautiful. She was who she was, take it or leave it. Mami loved her for that (and for her utter disrespect for my father).

While Kiki was quietly making the first *café con leche* of the day, Dulce began her workday by banging the pots as loudly as she could to wake and annoy my father. This was my cue to rush to the kitchen. I would come in, sit down, and be very still (she allowed me to stay in the kitchen but I couldn't move around). While I watched her cook, she would tell me stories. Fantastic stories, legends, really, about mythical people who were both men and women at the same time, who held conversations with vegetables and could conjure terrifying storms just by imagining them. I was spellbound. Telling one story after the next, stirring here, cutting there, never tiring, extracting good behavior from me with the promise of letting me know how the adventure at hand ended, Dulce would weave her magic, seducing me with *patakís,* the myths of the Santería pantheon. She insisted I learn the food preferences of all the *orishás* (deities). It would come in handy at the time of making offerings to praise, appease, or beg a favor from the saint.

Like any oral history, the stories often changed with each telling, but it was Dulce who made them come to life, playing all the characters in a scene, changing voices, gesticulating and dancing when she wanted to emphasize a point.

In addition to her storytelling flair, Dulce was an excellent cook with a special talent for frying—an essential skill in a Cuban kitchen. One of her specialties was fritters and she never made *calabaza* fritters without telling the story of how Ochún, the goddess of love, came to love Calabaza. Suffice it to say that money, talking *calabazas,* drunkenness, and adultery played a role.

Dulce made the lightest and tastiest fritters of anyone we knew. Fritters were served as a side dish at most meals and they ran the gamut of vegetables and tubers, savory mostly but sometimes sweet with sugarcane molasses for dessert. When dinner was almost ready my mother would say to Dulce, *"puede empezar a freir,"* you may begin to fry. The frying was always done at the last possible moment and only after everyone was at the table. These *calabaza* fritters are perfect with just about anything, but especially with a fiery oxtail stew or juicy pork chops. The recipe can be halved.

Frituras de Calabaza (Calabaza Fritters)

3 pounds calabaza (Caribbean pumpkin)
1 cinnamon stick
1 star anise
2 tablespoons dark brown sugar
1 tablespoon melted unsalted butter
1 large egg, slightly beaten
Pinch of salt
1 cup flour
1 tablespoon plus 1 teaspoon baking powder
Vegetable oil for frying

Preheat the oven to 350°F. Wash the calabaza, cut into chunks, and remove the seeds and strings. Place in an ovenproof pan with about ½ inch water, and place the cinnamon and star anise in the water. Sprinkle the calabaza with brown sugar, reserving 1 teaspoon for the dough. Bake until very tender, about 1 hour. Drain, discarding all liquid, cinnamon, and star anise. Peel the calabaza, place into a food processor, and process to make a thin puree. Measure 2 cups puree, transfer to a large bowl, and allow to cool completely.

To the puree add the melted butter, egg, salt, and the reserved teaspoon brown sugar and mix well. Sift the flour and baking powder together and mix thoroughly. Allow the dough to rest about 30 minutes before frying.

In a deep, heavy cast iron skillet or Dutch oven heat 2 to 3 inches oil to medium-high (375°F). Fill a teaspoon with dough and push into the hot oil with the help of another spoon. If the first fritter spreads out, add a little more flour. The flour-to-calabaza ratio is not exact, as some calabazas contain more water than others. Repeat to adjust. Cook in batches, making sure the skillet is not overcrowded, as this will create steam. Move the oil around with the back of a slotted spoon and turn the fritters over to brown on all sides, about 3 to 4 minutes. They should be golden. Drain over paper towels and keep warm until ready to serve.

Frituritas de Malanga (Malanga Fritters)

Malanga is a tuber also known as *yautía,* taro, or dasheen. It is dark brown and hairy on the outside and very white inside. It looks like a misshapen, elongated potato. *Malanga* fritters are always referred to in the diminutive and affectionately: We treasure them. A good *friturita de malanga* recipe might very well define a cook. Always present are garlic and parsley, except of course when the *frituritas* are made for dessert, served with thick sugarcane molasses. Everyone agrees that they must be made with raw *malanga* grated by hand, but if you insist, they could be grated finely and quickly (so as not to turn gummy) in a food processor. Dulce's recipe adds the disputed teaspoon of vinegar which I find essential for the crispness of the *friturita.*

The fritters were made small so they would easily cook through and they came to the table all crispy, crunchy, crusty, crackling, golden, but soft inside. It was always a battle between greed and good sense; you wanted to pop them in your mouth immediately even if it meant getting burned.

4 medium malangas (about 2 pounds)
2 eggs, slightly beaten
2 garlic cloves, pressed or minced
2 tablespoons minced parsley
1 teaspoon salt
1 teaspoon white vinegar
Oil for frying

Cut the *malangas* in half to make them easier to peel. Grate very finely on the fine side of a hand grater. Place in a bowl with all the ingredients except the oil and mix with a fork.

Allow to rest for about 15 minutes. If the dough seems too loose, add more grated *malanga*. Heat the oil and proceed to fry as instructed in the calabaza fritter recipe, page 48.

ARAÑITAS (SMALL SPIDERS)

Another option is Arañitas (small spiders). The proportions stay basically the same but the *malanga* is coarsely grated. When fried at 400°F, they open up to look something like a cobweb. They should be deep golden brown and very crisp. A terrific snack with drinks.

Dulce's Tips for Perfect Fritters

• Allow the dough to rest for an average of 15 minutes.

• Use clean vegetable oil—the same oil can be refrigerated and used again for fritters, but don't use it more than three or four times.

• Heat the oil in a deep, heavy cast iron skillet or Dutch oven.

• Make fritters small—use a teaspoon.

• If the first fritters spread out in the hot oil, add a little flour or more of the grated vegetable you are using to make a firmer dough; recipes cannot be absolutely exact as the texture of the vegetables is not consistent.

• Cook in batches, making sure the skillet is not over-crowded, as this will create steam.

SIX

The Enchantress

Pupen wore half a yard of Bakelite bracelets on each arm and rattled them constantly. I loved to hear the dry "rack rack" noise they made as she talked with her hands to make a point. She always wore small turbans close to her head (which of course matched her outfit) and she had a very personal aroma—a discreet sandalwood fragrance from Maja soap mingled with her Myrurgia foundation and a hint of tobacco from the Pall Malls (cadged from my father) she smoked, lighting one with another—noticeable even at a distance. Her smell had a comforting effect on me, like everything else about her. She had a large bosom, an old-fashioned monolithic mound that began under her arms and continued in one solid mass to her waist. She was of an undetermined age (older than my mother, but not as old as Abuela Monona, who was *very* old). Of medium height, she held herself straight, proud, like the stunning *trigueña* (brunette) she must have been once.

Any afternoon I was bored, or when my mom had had enough of me, I was sent to the parlor to talk to Papi's clients. It was during one of these attempts at socialization that I met Pupen, patiently waiting to have a *consulta* with my father.

Her real name was Fulgencia, same as Batista in the feminine, but I couldn't pronounce the "f" so she became Pupencia, Pupen for short. Even before I knew her name, my heart was hers. Gradually we became friends. Pupen came to see my father often, and I began inviting her to my room to play with my dolls. My mother, curious about this woman who seemed to have infinite patience and could keep me entertained for hours, began to make small talk with her and they immediately hit it off. My mom had been orphaned at the age of thirteen and she saw in Pupen the infinite tenderness and immense capacity to love she had been deprived of all her life. But most important, Pupen made her laugh.

How Pupen eventually came to live with us was never clear to me, but she became my principal nurturer and my mother's best friend. She told me stories of her days as a rural school inspector, about her travails in the countryside, about her work with the *campesino* children, stories so funny and so fantastic I didn't believe them. But they were actually true, or mostly true, just somewhat embellished for a better punchline.

My favorite, which she told again and again at my request, was her story about the oxcart that got stuck in the mud when she was trying to reach a distant, rural school. In one telling, extraterrestrials rolled the cart out of the mud with just one touch to the *yunque.* In another version, a flock of Persian angels rescued the cart, batting their wings so hard the mud slid away and dried. Once it was the Aviator from the newly published (1943) *Little Prince,* who lassoed the cart from his airplane and flew high, so high that the cart practically left the earth. Or the Magi appeared and enchanted the oxen, giving them extraordinary strength to pull the cart free. They, the Magi, always arrived with pencils and notebooks for all the children (this version came with an admonition to be grateful for all we had).

Pupen was an expert on the *charada* (an elaborate numbers system corresponding to animals and objects) and loved to interpret Mami's dreams by choosing the number that represented whatever Mami had dreamt about. They would then play these numbers on Saturday mornings with Ramón, the neighborhood numbers runner, presenting him with a piece of paper with the numbers carefully written in Pupen's impeccable hand and the money neatly folded inside. She and Mami went fifty-fifty, and they always won. The winnings were never large, since their bets never exceeded a dollar or two. It was just for fun and to see if Pupen's hunches were right.

My mother trusted Pupen and confided in her, and Pupen gave her an amount of stability she desperately needed in the middle of our chaotic household. Pupen had lived a large life and her fortunes had changed several times, but she wasn't bitter or disillusioned. She accepted that life was disappointing and took her knocks in elegant stride. She was a woman of the world and possessed a dignity that my mother held in great respect. In the same way some women feed their families with food, Pupen provided my mother and me with spiritual and emotional sustenance—through her stories, her love, her strength, and principally her sense of humor. Her philosophy was that life and everything in it was impermanent, so why suffer by getting attached to any particular outcome? Things would change soon enough.

Pupen rarely went out on her own because I couldn't bear to be without her. She would get all dressed up, matching shoes to bag, carefully pulling up her silk stockings and affixing them to her garters. I would watch her put on her makeup, the powder that smelled like her and that dark red lipstick I envied, wishing I too could wear it to be more like her. Her bracelets went on next, her turban last. As she left, I would watch her from the *balcón*, my hands tight around the wrought iron bars, until she disappeared around the corner. I always cried. It broke my heart to see her walk away. And it broke her heart too. She just couldn't stand for me to be sad. More often than not, she turned around and came right back, forgetting why she was going out in the first place.

If she did manage to complete an outing, she consoled me by bringing home a box of my favorite sweets or better still, making me a coconut flan. And we knew each time, she and I belonged to each other.

When I decided to be baptized I chose her to be my godmother. And in truth, other than my crush on Father José María, the only reason I wanted to be baptized was to be related to Pupen. I wanted our love for each other to be recognized and formalized. We were now not only family of the heart, but family in the eyes of the Church.

Flan de Coco
(Coconut Flan)

As a conciliatory gesture nothing was better than my *madrina's* coconut flan. Pupen wasn't much of a cook herself, taking a more literary place in the family, but she had perfected a few dishes and this is one of them. She is in my heart, and whenever I make this flan it's with a sad smile on my face. She made it for me with love and care and I miss all that.

For the Caramel
½ cup sugar

For the Flan
2 large eggs
4 large egg yolks
One 16-ounce can shredded coconut in heavy syrup
1 tablespoon dark, aromatic rum

To make the caramel, stir ¼ cup water and sugar to dissolve in a small, heavy saucepan. Place over high heat and cook without stirring until the sugar begins to turn brown, or caramelize. When it is golden brown, carefully pour it into a 1 quart rectangular (10 x 4 x 3 inches) paté mold or 4 cup capacity round mold. Use oven mitts to hold the mold and turn it to coat the bottom and sides with the caramel. Set aside.

To make the flan, preheat the oven to 325°F. Slightly beat the whole eggs and yolks together and strain through a fine mesh sieve into a bowl. This will ensure a smooth flan. Pour in the shredded coconut with its syrup, add the rum, and stir to mix well.

Pour the flan mixture into the prepared mold and place the mold in a hot water bath—a larger pan filled with enough hot but not boiling water to come three-quarters up the mold. Place in the middle rack of the oven and bake for 1 hour and 30 minutes. Place on a rack to cool slightly and refrigerate for a minimum of 4 hours before serving.

To unmold, run a sharp knife along the edges of the flan, dip in a pan of hot water for few seconds, place a serving platter over the mold, and invert. Place the empty mold in hot water again to soften the rest of the caramel and pour over the flan.

SEVEN

The Convert

Love made me a Catholic. Throughout my childhood, my cousins Nene and Lilian lived with my grandparents down the street from our house. They were sixteen and seventeen, and looked like sophisticated women to a girl of seven. I loved being around them and would do anything to do so. That included going to mass every Sunday at La Iglesia del Carmen, a magnificent colonial church a few blocks away from our home. Masses were quite a production then, clouds of incense, *kyrie eleisons* and *mea culpas* in Latin with a conglomeration of acolytes. The priests faced the altar, their backs to the congregation, and only at certain parts of the ritual did they turn around. It was during one of those moments I got my first glimpse of Padre José María, and it was love at first sight.

One look at the young padre and I was an instant convert. Suddenly I loved mass, the Church, and everything that went along with being Catholic. I wanted to participate in all of the mysteries of the Church, to go to confession (I had no idea what it was), and receive communion. But there was a problem. I was seven years old and I had not been baptized. Since most Cuban children were baptized when they were only a few days old, to ensure their little baby souls wouldn't be hanging around in limbo, my situation was unusual. My father, the freethinker, thought that everyone should be allowed to choose their own beliefs, and I would, in due time, be able to make an informed decision about religion. Therefore, there was no timely baptism for me.

My cousins, already scandalized by the state of my soul, diligently and in great scary detail explained to me that I was a heathen and therefore could never go to Heaven. Worse, unless I made my first communion, I would never be able to receive the coveted communion wafer from the hands of Padre José María. But even before I could take communion, I had to be baptized.

That did it. Being banned from Heaven was okay by me, angels flapping their wings and playing the harp didn't sound like too much fun, but the separation from the padre was more than my innocent passion could take. I asked my father to have me baptized on two non-negotiable conditions: I was to choose my godmother (my beloved Pupen) and Padre José María was to perform the ceremony. And so it was. Love made me a Catholic.

After the baptism, my cousin Nene, who had always spoiled me, seemed to spoil me even more. She was happy to take me to mass every Sunday and I was happy to see Padre José María. After mass, as a reward, Nene would take me home with her and let me help her cook. Since it was the cook's day off, we had the kitchen to ourselves. Nene's specialty was desserts; bread pudding (as taught by Abuela Monona), flan, *buñuelos*, her custards and meringues were absolutely magnificent. She beat, I stirred. When she finished folding in the egg whites I licked the bowl. I watched the caramel; she poured it. I prepared the hot water bath or *bain marie*; she put it in the oven. It was sheer joy. No wonder I loved her so much and no wonder still I associate mass with lust and gluttony, two of the seven cardinal sins.

Merengón Cubano (Cuban Floating Island)

This is an old Cuban recipe which appears in every family's recipe book. It is mostly reserved for special occasions and does make a very special entrance. This is my cousin Nene's version with a couple of additions from me.

For the Caramel
¾ cup sugar
2 tablespoons candied ginger, finely chopped

For the Meringue
¾ cup egg whites, approximately 6 large egg whites
5 tablespoons sugar
3 tablespoons candied ginger, finely chopped

For the Light Custard
2 cups milk
½ cup sugar
6 large egg yolks
1 teaspoon dark aromatic rum
½ teaspoon vanilla extract

Preheat the oven to 300°F. In a heavy saucepan, boil the sugar and ¼ cup water together to make a caramel. Sprinkle the candied ginger on the bottom of an 8 inch ring mold and pour in the caramel to coat. Set aside.

For the meringue, beat the egg whites to soft peaks in an electric mixer. Gradually add the sugar while continuing to beat to stiff peaks. Add the candied ginger a little at a time while the machine is still on to incorporate evenly. Carefully transfer the meringue to the caramelized mold and tap gently to settle the meringue.

Turn the oven down to 250°F. Place the meringue in a hot water bath—a larger pan filled with enough hot but not boiling water to come up within 1 inch of the top. Place on the middle rack of the oven and bake for 1 hour and 30 minutes or until the meringue is springy but still soft to the touch. Allow to cool before unmolding.

While the meringue is baking, make the light custard. Bring the milk to a boil in a heavy saucepan and in a bowl cream the egg yolks and sugar together until pale yellow. Add half the hot milk to the egg mixture and stir well. Pour the mixture back into the saucepan and continue to cook very gently while stirring until the sauce coats the back of a wooden spoon. Use a heat diffuser if necessary to prevent curdling.

Transfer the custard to a cool bowl and stir in the rum and vanilla. If the sauce should curdle, give it a few whizzes in a food processor. Pour the sauce in a deep serving dish and unmold the meringue ring on top.

EIGHT

The Aerialist

In a ritzier family, Kiki would have been the majordomo or even the housekeeper, with keys to the wine cellar and silver vault hanging from his belt. For us he was the general factotum whose title of "assistant" to my father belied the fact that he ran all of our errands and tended to the chores around the house that my mother wouldn't touch. He sewed on buttons, hemmed dresses, and ironed the fine linens that could not be trusted to the laundress.

He came to us through my father's parents. Kiki's mother had made him leave home because he was gay. He lived in our neighborhood (we lived at the end of the block from my grandparents) and the *Abuelos* had given him refuge and a room above the garage. When *Abuelito* Don Pancho died, Kiki became my father's responsibility.

Kiki, an amiable sort, agreeable and gracious, was very tall and thin but quite strong. He had been a trapeze artist in a rural circus and had toured the island end to end playing every town that had more than one street and a mayor. Other than swinging around without a net, his most important duty in the circus was to take care of everyone's costumes. So it followed when he came to us, he became my mother's fashion consultant. It had been his idea to dye her hair mahogany red and for her to wear only solid colors. Both had been very successful suggestions. My mother was thought of as *muy elegante.* Kiki's principal duty in our household, however, was to make the first *café con leche* of the morning.

Another of Kiki's duties, even if unofficial, was to pamper me and keep me occupied, which he did with great delight. Sometimes in the middle of the afternoon when the household was quiet and Dulce was resting, Kiki would call me into the kitchen in a loud stage whisper. In silence, he would make a small potato or sweet plantain *tortilla* in a little cast iron skillet that had belonged to Abuela Monona (she had used it to fry her perfect eggs, one at a time); it was just the right size for a small omelet for two.

When there was enough time, meaning no one was going to interrupt us, Kiki would make churros and hot *chocolate a la Española,* thick and dark. We would share that too, eating fast, in silence, like a great pantomime, selfishly hoping no one would come by so we wouldn't have to part with even with one precious bite. It made us conspirators and it made us friends.

Kiki's Ritualistic Café con Leche

As soon as the milk was delivered in the morning he poured it into a large pot, added a generous pinch of salt, and set about boiling it several times. These were the days before pasteurized milk, so boiling was an important process and there was a definite ritual to it. When the milk rose the first time, the pot was removed from the burner and the milk aerated with a large ladle. This process was repeated several times until there was lots of froth and Kiki was completely sure the milk was safe to drink.

Then came the coffee.

Ample water was boiled until large bubbles formed. The boiled water was then slowly poured, in a circular motion, over the ground coffee placed in the *manga,* a funnel-shaped cloth, held over a pitcher. To be correct the coffee had to be very strong, and normally the water would be sugared, though Kiki made it without sugar, the way my mother liked it.

Then came the fine tuning.

Kiki took pride in knowing exactly how everyone in the house liked their *café con leche.* He never had to ask. Ours being such an extended household, this was quite a feat. Some preferred more coffee than milk and others allowed just enough milk in their coffee to be able to claim they were indeed drinking *café con leche* and not *café solo.* Then there were those who went for strictly half-and-half, sweetened to the point of syrup, or the purists who took absolutely no sugar. Regardless, Kiki knew the perfect combination. The only proper accompaniment for the morning *café con leche* was *tostadas.* But that was already Dulce's territory.

Chocolate con Churros
(Hot Chocolate and Churros)

There is a saying *"las cosas claras y el chocolate a la española,"* meaning keep things clear and my chocolate Spanish style. The hot chocolate in Spain is served as thick as a loose mousse, the better to dip your churros in, using the churros as a spoon. That was the way we liked it and the way Kiki made it.

Churros

8 tablespoons (1 stick) unsalted melted butter
1 teaspoon salt
½ cup all-purpose flour
8 cups vegetable oil for frying
1 cup granulated sugar, for rolling
1 cup water

To make the churro dough, heat 1 cup water, the butter, and salt to a rolling boil in a 3-quart saucepan. Add the flour and stir vigorously over low heat until mixture forms a ball, approximately 1 minute, and remove from heat. Continue to beat until smooth.

Heat the oil in a deep frying pan to 360°F.

Spoon the dough into a piping bag with a star tip. Squeeze 6-inch strips of dough into the hot oil. Fry three or four strips at a time until golden brown, turning once, about 2 minutes on each side. Drain on paper towels. Roll the churros in the sugar. Don't let them wait to be eaten, or they'll go soggy on you.

Hot Chocolate

6 ounces dark bittersweet chocolate (70% cacao bean)
4 cups whole milk
1 tablespoon cornstarch
3 tablespoons sugar, or more to taste if drinking alone (if drinking
   with churros, use little or no sugar)

Grate the chocolate on the coarse side of a hand grater. Place the
chocolate and half the milk in a saucepan over very low heat and
cook, stirring until the chocolate has melted. Stir the cornstarch
into the remaining milk to dissolve and whisk into the chocolate
with the sugar. Cook on low heat, whisking constantly until the
chocolate thickens, about 5 minutes. Remove from the heat and
whisk until thick, smooth, and shiny. Serve with churros.

Tortilla de Plátanos Maduros (Ripe Plantain Omelet)

A popular dish which became conspiratorial in Kiki's hands.

1 very ripe plantain
Olive oil for frying
5 large eggs
Salt and freshly ground black pepper to taste

Peel the plantain and cut into ¼-inch slices. Heat the oil in a nonstick skillet and fry the plantains at medium heat until golden brown and cooked through. Remove the plantain and keep warm. Discard the oil or save for another use, leaving about 1 tablespoon in the skillet.

Beat the eggs vigorously with the salt and pepper. Add the cooked plantains to the eggs and pour into the skillet, arranging the plantains so they do not overlap. Cook at a gentle heat while shaking the pan so the *tortilla* doesn't stick. Push in the edges with a wooden spoon to evenly distribute the eggs. When the eggs begin to set, place a large plate over the pan, and with a quick movement flip the *tortilla* onto the plate so the bottom of the *tortilla* is face up. Slide the tortilla back into the pan and cook the underside, continuing to shake the pan until the *tortilla* is done. Let the *tortilla* set for a few minutes before cutting.

NINE

Saturday Mornings with Ramón, Don Juan, and Doña Pastorita

Ramón

Saturday mornings were busier than usual at home. There was a party atmosphere. Ramón was a regular fixture and while waiting for my father to give him his bets, he'd go to the kitchen and get a platter from a hesitant Dulce to serve the guava pasties he had brought us.

Ramón was Pupen's black-sheep brother. He had gone to university to become an attorney, but in his last year took up with a rough crowd and gambled away what little he had, even pawning his law books for extra cash. I think he never recovered and was actually in the business to cover his own bets.

He was a sweet guy, always in an impeccably ironed *guayabera*, his hair slicked back, with the easy laughter and effortless charm of the born con man. My dad admired him for his unapologetic ways.

Both my mom and Pupen were regulars of his, betting on *la charada* numbers or buying a "special" lottery ticket. For them, being with Ramón was more about the social interchange and the innocent neighborhood gossip than anything else. I remember them sitting around the dining room table talking loudly and laughing hard all at the same time, like we Cubans do. I loved that, and I especially liked it when Ramón would go on and on about *la charada,* and its symbols.

La Charada

La bolita, another name for *la charada,* was an illegal game of numbers, and half the fun of playing and perhaps guessing the number or numbers of the day was precisely because it was against the law. The system had come to Cuba as *chiflá* with the Chinese immigrants of the nineteenth century. The figure of a traditionally dressed Chinese man was illustrated with numbers from one to thirty-six corresponding to different parts of the body and/or different animals. Number one was represented by a horse and it rested on top of the head of the figure. Thirty-five represented a spider on the left wrist; the rat, number twenty-nine, was on the left ankle and so on. But thirty-six numbers seemed too few for Cubans and with their popular creativity, they proceeded to add another sixty-four to make an even hundred. These numbers correspond to new objects, such as a ring, a bed, a ship, and to states of being, like drunk, crazy, stabbed, or married. There were new animals like mosquitoes, sharks, turtles, and bats too; and if you shook a scorpion from your boot, you had to play number forty-three.

Pastelitos de Guayaba (Guava Pasties)

Mostly guava *pastelitos* were store bought, a very sweet guava paste wrapped in flaky pastry, and still are sold in every *cafecito* and Cuban bakery in Miami. While I like the classic phyllo dough effect, I've always found the store-bought variety cloyingly sweet. So to satisfy my cravings and my taste I came up with an easy recipe. Mine are more *empanaditas* than *pastelitos.* By whatever name, I find them irresistible. Each time I bite into one, I am transported to the unofficial party being held at our dining room table every Saturday morning in La Habana.

> *2 rounds store-bought refrigerated pie dough (I prefer Pillsbury)*
> *4 ounces guava paste (see sidebar), cut into ¼-inch-thick, ½-inch-long strips*
> *1 egg, slightly beaten with cream, milk, or water*

Preheat the oven to 350°F. Roll out the dough on a floured surface to about ⅛ inch thick. With a cookie cutter or the top of a drinking glass, cut the dough into small circles, about 2 inches in diameter.

Place a strip of the guava paste just below the center of each circle. Moisten the borders with water. Bring the longer top to cover the guava paste and press to close. Press again with the tines of a fork. Make sure to moisten the fork in water so it doesn't stick.

Make two or three tiny vents on the pasties (or they'll explode) and brush with the egg mixture. Place on a cookie sheet and bake for 10 to 12 minutes, until golden. Serve warm.

Before baking, the pasties can be frozen on a flat surface. When completely frozen, transfer to a plastic bag.

Makes about 30 pasties.

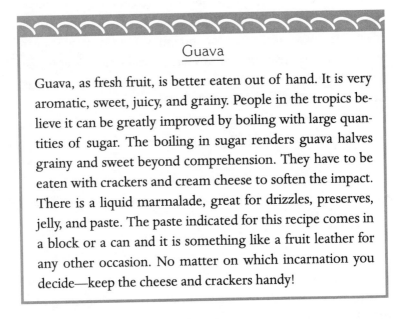

Guava

Guava, as fresh fruit, is better eaten out of hand. It is very aromatic, sweet, juicy, and grainy. People in the tropics believe it can be greatly improved by boiling with large quantities of sugar. The boiling in sugar renders guava halves grainy and sweet beyond comprehension. They have to be eaten with crackers and cream cheese to soften the impact. There is a liquid marmalade, great for drizzles, preserves, jelly, and paste. The paste indicated for this recipe comes in a block or a can and it is something like a fruit leather for any other occasion. No matter on which incarnation you decide—keep the cheese and crackers handy!

Don Juan and Joselito

Don Juan, who had once been a carpenter, was old and very thin, dark skinned with a white stubble and a buzz cut. Joselito was his black and white fox terrier mix, and they adored each other. Don Juan and his dog came to visit on Saturday mornings without fail. He knew he could count on a good breakfast for them both. Besides Kiki's *café con leche* and Ramón's *pastelitos,* my father would send Kiki to buy several *fritas* (Cuban hamburgers) for both of them.

Don Juan and his dog came to us by way of one of my father's post-hurricane excursions through Havana and Las Llaguas, one of Havana's poorest shantytowns, where he found Don Juan. Apparently Don Juan had hung a handmade sign, *Carpintero,* in front of his shack where he sat in a rickety chair, and Papi was moved by the man's desire to work. He brought Don Juan (who would not go anywhere without Joselito) home and found him something to do. Don Juan refused to accept any handouts; he liked to work for whatever he received. I felt very privileged when he allowed me to feed Joselito and play with him.

Frita Habanera (Havana Burger)

The *frita* was by definition small, so to say that Don Juan and Joselito could easily put away six at one sitting is not really saying much. By virtue of being a popular dish, *frita* recipes abound, with bread, without, with chorizo or not. This very simple version is the one I like to make, but I tart it up with a very untraditional *schmear* of mayonnaise mixed with hot *pimentón*.

8 small hamburger buns

For the Fritas
1 pound ground beef
8 ounces ground fully cooked Spanish chorizo
1 teaspoon salt
½ teaspoon freshly ground black pepper
2 tablespoons oil for frying

To Finish
4 tablespoons mayonnaise
1 teaspoon or less hot pimentón to taste
2 cans matchstick potatoes

Preheat the oven to 300°F to warm up the buns while preparing and cooking the *fritas*. Combine all the *frita* ingredients in a bowl except for the oil and mix well, using your hands. Shape the meat into balls about 1 inch in circumference and flatten slightly. Heat the oil in a large skillet and cook at medium heat 3 to 4 minutes on each side. Gently flatten the *fritas* with the spatula as they cook.

To finish, mix the mayonnaise and *pimentón* together. Remove the buns from the oven and spread both top and bottom halves with the spicy mayo. Place the *frita* on the bottom half of the roll and heap with the potatoes. Press to close. For a more traditional *frita* you can leave out the mayo and just spread a little ketchup on the bun.

Pastorita

Doña Pastorita, as I was supposed to respectfully call our land-lady, it had been said was retired from the oldest profession and lived in total seclusion in the downstairs level of the once great but now decaying house we rented. She had been a great beauty and in her day had caught the eye of a cabinet minister who set her up in this house and left it to her upon his death.

Most mornings we heard her start the day by reprimanding her young country maid for not making the *cafecito* with the proper foam. Sometimes on Saturdays, when the pandemonium at home was at its height, I would slip downstairs unnoticed. At Doña Pastorita's everything was quiet, and she would be dressed and made up as if she were going to a party, no matter how early in the day. This fascinated me and I would stop by just to see Doña Pastorita sitting there with her powdered pale face, her dark red lipstick, and her flawlessly coiffed black-as-a-crow's-wing hair.

In her home everything had a place and everything was in the same place every time I visited. She had carefully tended potted plants in the interior patio and her kitchen was spotless; pots and pans were polished and put away. Her dressing table was immaculate, all her creams in a neat row, her powder to the right of her tubes of lipstick, equidistant from the edge of the dresser; on the other side sat her clean brush and comb. This type of precise placement and neatness was so different from what it was at home. For one, Mami did not have a dressing table.

Doña Pastorita would take my short visits as an opportunity to teach me things that I would later need in life, like, how to make the proper *cafecito* and light a cigar.

I was no Gigi, but her instructions were not entirely wasted.

How to Cut and Light a Cigar

Doña Pastorita taught me that the better the cigar (and she wouldn't know anyone who didn't smoke the best), the more important the cut. The object was to create an ample, smooth opening to draw from without hurting the structure of the cigar.

This means cutting part of the cap (the leaf that closes the cigar at the top) to a rounded point 2 or 3 millimeters from where the cigar starts to straighten out. Using a proper cigar cutter is the best way to create a large, exposed surface that will allow an even draw and a proper burn. Doña Pastorita insisted that the only way to light a cigar was with a butane gas lighter. Anything else, a candle or matches, would affect the taste of the cigar. The trick is to hold the cigar above the flame without touching it and patiently rotate it until a glowing, even ring appears at the end. (To me this phase of the ritual was the most fun.) Then and only then is the cigar ready to offer its sensual first puff.

Cafecito con Espumita (Cuban Coffee with Foam)

We made coffee in the cloth *manga,* but I can replicate the results using a standard Italian espresso maker. The trick to the foam, and what makes it authentic, is to place as much sugar as you want per *demi tasse,* usually 1 teaspoon in one single cup. The moment the coffee starts brewing, when it gives its first spurt, place 2 or 3 drops—any amount larger than drops will not give you the desired result—in the cup with the sugar. Start stirring madly until you have a cream. When the coffee is ready, pour the coffee down the side of the cup into the sugar cream in order to make perfect foam.

TEN

Pilgrimage to Regla

The black Virgen de Regla in Chipiona, a small coastal village near Cádiz, Spain, has mysterious origins. The legend claims that the Virgin has African origins—that Saint Augustine himself, as Bishop of Hippo in North Africa in the fourth and fifth centuries, had commissioned her image to be carved out of a solid piece of wood. Later he sent the statue to Spain for protection from the vandals, but no one knew the fate of the statue. In the thirteenth century, by a "miracle," the statue was found in Chipiona well hidden from view by a fig tree. Since then the Virgen de Regla has made her home in Chipiona in a beautiful sanctuary by the sea. Eventually her devotion reached Havana through the Augustine brothers and her depository was a hamlet at the entrance of the Bay of Havana. As the hamlet grew, it adopted the name of the Virgin, Regla. Here she had a view of the ocean too.

Upon arrival in Cuba, la Virgen de Regla's legend grew even more extraordinary. She became part of the Santería pantheon and merged with the powerful African deity Yemayá, the mother of all life. Yemayá counted Dulce among her more devoted daughters and as such Dulce kept a small shrine for her in our kitchen. Everything Dulce cooked was blessed by Yemayá. For a long time Dulce had wanted to introduce me to Yemayá, La Virgen de Regla, in person. I didn't quite understand what she meant, but I was eager to go on any adventure with her. Dulce was incredibly persuasive and after months of trying, finally got permission from my mother to take me to Yemaya's sanctuary, la Virgen de Regla Chapel.

In order to reach the town of Regla we had to travel across the Bay of Havana in the *lanchita*, a sputtering ferry (a very fitting vehicle for the goddess of the sea). On that day, a Friday (Yemayá's favorite day), we boarded the brightly painted ferry and sat to the side so we would get wet with the sea spray. The church, as well as most of Regla, was built on the side of a hill close to the water with an ample view of the bay. It was not an imposing church in size or treasure. It was modest, humble even, magnificent only in the devotion of its people to the black Madonna.

The image of the Virgin herself, placed in the center of the main altar, was not very large. She wore a white gown draped with a midnight blue cape that twinkled with tiny stars and a tall crown encrusted with semiprecious stones. La Virgen stood on a crescent moon with a halo of golden rays all around her and held a standing white baby Jesus on her lap. Her countenance was peaceful and sweet. It was easy for me to see why this particular saint in the guise of Yemayá was acclaimed as the mother of all, of having power over the moon and all female mysteries, maternity, conception, and childbirth. She was the ruler of the oceans.

I was overwhelmed with love when I saw her. She was so beautiful, so delicate, so gentle and kind. She looked right into my eyes, and I wanted her to hold me in her arms, to comfort me. I understood why Dulce loved this Virgin so much, why she softened when she spoke of Yemayá. Dulce saw I now understood everything, even how La Virgen de Regla and Yemayá could be one and the same. She put her arm around my shoulders and drew me closer.

As an offering, we had brought Yemayá's favorite foods, plantain chips and pork cracklings, black-eyed pea fritters and half a watermelon cut in slices, which Dulce had carefully and gently prepared that morning. When it was time, we sang a little song to her in the yoruba language, Lucumí.

Mariquitas

Universal in the Spanish-speaking Caribbean, plantain chips are claimed as their own by each and every single island. They've spread all over and you are just as likely to find them in chic establishments as in the corner bodega. The truth is there couldn't be a simpler and tastier alternative to potato chips. Eat them with consciousness of making an offering to Yemayá.

> *1 large very green plantain*
> *Canola oil for frying*
> *Sea salt to taste*

To peel the green plantain, slice off the ends and cut the plantain in half. Make two lengthwise slits at the natural ridges of the skin, cutting through to the flesh. Lift the skin away with the edge of the knife, pulling across rather than lengthwise.

Into a large, deep pot (a Dutch oven is ideal), pour about 2 inches oil and heat to 375°F.

While the oil heats, slice the plantain very thin with a mandoline (if available) or, with a very sharp, thin knife, slice as thinly as you can. The slices should be thin enough to be translucent. Keep in a bowl of cold water with a squint of lemon juice to avoid discoloration. If using a mandoline slice directly into the hot oil. Pat dry. Place the chips in the oil one right after another or they will stick together. Work quickly or they will burn. Swirl the oil with the back of a slotted spoon to keep them moving and as soon as the chips turn yellow, drain on paper towels.

Salt generously with sea salt. Once they have completely cooled they can be saved in an open paper bag and reheated later in a medium oven in the same bag.

Fiery Chicken Breasts with Sautéed Sweet Apples for Changó

Changó, an important Santería deity, is omnivorous and very partial to all fowl and lamb. He loves cornflour and apples, dried fish, red wine, and rum. His favorite offering is an apple with drizzled honey; he may be inclined to bring sweetness to your affairs. His color is red, his instrument the drums. He rules the dance and is a very virile deity, a man's man. He is irascible, capricious, and has many a contradictory *pataki*, the myths that describe the deity and its powers. One *pataki* states that Ochún, La Virgen de la Caridad del Cobre, was his birth mother and that Yemayá had raised him as her son. Another says his birth mother was Obatalá, La Señora de la Mercedes, and it was Ochún who raised him. Yet another has Ochún, Obatalá, and Yemayá living together and Changó coming to scold them for an infraction toward Elegguá, guardian of all doors and roads. And one better still, along the Oedipus line, involving Yemayá.

For the Chicken
2 skinless, boneless chicken breasts, cut in half and lightly flattened
2 tablespoons flour
1 teaspoon salt
Freshly ground black pepper to taste
¼ teaspoon hot pimentón
2 tablespoons vegetable oil

For the Apples
2 tablespoons sweet butter
2 Gala or Fuji apples, thinly sliced

1 tablespoon dark honey
2 tablespoons dark rum

Rinse the chicken breasts and pat dry with paper towels. Combine the flour with the seasonings and lightly dust the chicken breasts with this mixture.

In a nonstick frying pan just large enough to hold the chicken breasts without overlapping, heat the oil at medium-high heat. Place the chicken in the pan and brown well on both sides, about 3 minutes on each side. Turn the heat down and cook for about 8 minutes total, depending on the thickness of the breast, or until the juices run clear when pricked with a fork.

Drain the chicken breasts on paper towels and keep warm.

To the same pan, add the butter and sauté the apple slices at medium-high heat for about 3 minutes until slightly soft. Drizzle the honey over the apples and shake the pan to evenly distribute. Add the rum and ignite. Cook for 1 additional minute.

Transfer the chicken breasts to a serving platter and place the apple slices around them to serve.

Santería

The Yoruba religion, or *la Regla de Ochá,* to use its correct name, came to Cuba with the African slaves who had been brought to work the sugarcane fields. Much of the Yoruba pantheon assumed specific Catholic saints' images and personalities to become Santería. To the Catholic practitioner, the image of the saint is the representation of a spiritual entity who lived as a human at some point in history. To the practitioner of Santería, the Catholic image of the saint is the embodiment of a Yoruba god. Santería in its purest form is a worship of the saints, a curious mix of magical African rites and traditions of the Catholic Church.

The *orishás* (deities) were matched to the Catholic saints by character traits and by similarities in image representations. For example, Yemayá was a fecund deity who ruled the waters, so the fact that La Virgen de Regla lived by the sea made her a logical match for Yemayá.

Changó, who had power over thunder and was both male and female, was paired off with Santa Barbara. In both representational images, the male Changó and female Santa Barbara wear crowns and carry arms; he, a double edged ax; she, a sword. She has been identified with storms and lightning; he rules fire, warriors, and violence. When Changó attacked he was implacable, but just like a tropical tempest, his fury was soon spent.

Changó is the most popular of the gods among Cubans, and some of the old *babalaos* (high priests of Santeria), say that it is because his character resembles the Cubans' so much. He loves to dance, drink, and eat, and he is a terror with women. Others claim that Changó is so popular because he is so feared. It is best to be on his good side, appeasing him daily with his favorite foods. Yemayá is the only one who can keep Changó in check. As terrifying as he is, he has to obey her, for she is one of his mothers.

Credit an open mind or the infinite capacity of Cubans for all things fantastic and implausible, there was absolutely no duality in this form of worship (except for the profoundly Catholic). Yemayá and the Virgen de Regla, Ochún and La Caridad del Cobre, Cuba's patron saint, Changó and Santa Barbara, were to most of us one and the same.

The Yoruba religion has a convoluted cosmology and an intricate pantheon. The gods' fickle and complicated lives rival any in Greek mythology. Precisely because these deities fought, womanized, ate, drank, and tricked each other, they seemed human and were that much more approachable as a result.

An *orishá*, so human in character, may also appear human in his needs, with well-defined tastes and preferences that may demand not only flowers and candles, but cigars and rum, as well as his favorite foods prepared a certain way. If you complied with the deity's wishes, you would be granted a special protection from evil, disease, and heartbreak, and be granted an abundance of health, wealth, and love. The relationships forged between gods and humans were familial ones with obligations on both sides.

There is at least one *pataki* for each *orishá* that justifies or explains in elaborate detail how each *orishá's* taste in a specific food came about. Those were the stories Dulce told me every day.

Yemayá

Yemaya's sacrificial animals are lamb and fowl, fish, turtles, and goats. Her offering foods include plantain chips, pork cracklings, and black-eyed peas. She likes her food liberally spread with sugarcane molasses. Yemayá's favorite fruit is the watermelon. Her water is seawater. A beautiful way to honor her is to bring white flowers to the ocean's edge and float them as you dedicate them to her.

Yemayá is summoned at the seashore with a gourd rattle. She is very graceful and carries a fan made of duck feathers. To dance she undulates her body, at first gently, growing slowly to a crescendo of waves in a storm.

Her colors are blue and white; her altar should be decorated with silver objects. She loves rings, seashells, starfish, and seahorses, anything that has to do with the ocean. All the offerings should be made in sets of seven, her favorite number. She likes her children to wear her necklaces of white and blue beads.

ELEVEN

The German Spy

Adolfina, who called herself Marguerite, and who may or may not have been a German spy, and may or may not have been a sailor, lived with us briefly in 1942 or 1943. This was during World War II, when Havana was crawling with spies and foreign operatives. My father had found her by the docks and brought her home with him in the middle of the night.

Early the next morning, when I went to the balcony as I always did to watch Kiki coming down the street, I saw a strange person sleeping on the floor in the living room out of the corner of my eye. I poked her and she didn't move. I ran to the back of the house screaming there was a dead person in the living room. Mami came to see what was going on and my dad lagged a few minutes behind. Mami and this person, now fully awake, could only look at each other silently, she with contempt, my mom with complete surprise.

When Papi started explaining her presence, he referred to her as a him, a sailor he had found unconscious, literally lying in a gutter by the docks. My father had brought "him" (the sailor) home to protect him from unknown evil.

Well, that story didn't go over too well, since it was obvious, despite the shaved head and the blue work shirt and pants, that this sailor was clearly a "her." I immediately disliked her and became jealous as I always did when a woman other than my mother came near my dad. Mami was astonished my father would do such a thing, but nevertheless agreed to give the woman refuge for a few days until she recovered from an ear infection.

We did not know her real name. We doubted it was really Marguerite, too delicate for such a rough customer, so we referred to her as Adolfina after Hitler. It turned out she played the piano divinely and would play Mozart for my mother. It seemed to soothe both of them.

Adolfina stayed well beyond her reluctant welcome, past a few days to a few weeks. Nobody in the household warmed up to her. Dulce, just as jealous as I, led the hate parade and would not allow her in the kitchen, not even for a glass of water. Communication was difficult. Adolfina actually spoke Spanish very well, but we made a point of not understanding her accent.

Christmas came and with it a tree and the promise of a crèche, which Mami never got around to assembling. Adolfina made it her job to set it up when no one was looking. She broke a mirror to make a stream, made *papier mâché* mountains, and conjured animals out of little bits of paper. It was the most beautiful crèche we had ever had. I hated it.

To make matters worse, she made pancakes for Christmas breakfast, an unforgivable infraction on Dulce's territory. By now I was intensely jealous of Adolfina, and in an altogether grumpy mood, irrationally fearing she could take my father away and destroy our family. Dulce threatened to put a curse on her if she didn't leave soon. It must have worked. Shortly after the pancake incident, Adolfina disappeared as mysteriously as she had appeared.

German Pancakes

I have no idea what made these pancakes so German, but since they were made by Marguerite a.k.a. Adolfina they were, by definition, German. I had noticed my mom, in spite of herself, taking notes in a corner. So over the years they have become "our" German pancakes. Well, they are baked in the oven, so I suppose that qualifies them as such.

1 cup all-purpose flour
1 teaspoon baking powder
Pinch of salt
2 tablespoons superfine sugar
2 large eggs, separated
¼ cup milk
2 tablespoons melted butter
Butter to grease the pan
Confectioners' sugar
Red currant jelly

Preheat the oven to 425°F. Sift the dry ingredients together into a large bowl. Add the egg yolks, milk, and melted butter. Blend well.

Beat the egg whites until they form soft peaks and gently fold them into the flour and milk mixture.

Butter an 8-inch square baking dish. Pour in the batter and tap to spread evenly.

Bake for 15 to 20 minutes until puffy and golden. Sprinkle confectioners' sugar on top, cut into portions, and serve immediately. Serve with red currant or loganberry jelly.

TWELVE

The Magical Kingdom

The drive to Boca Ciega was only thirty minutes long, up and down a narrow, winding road. From my perspective, piled in my dad's sweet two-toned Mercury Coupe along with my mom and my brothers, the trip seemed much longer. I just couldn't wait to get there. As we approached the last hill before reaching the beach, Papi would start revving us up with excitement about what we were about to see. He would stop the Coupe on the crest of the last hill before town, at the point where we could see the whole stretch of white sand and blue sea below, and would present the view like a gift to us. He and I would jump out of the car, fling open our arms, and sing at the tops of our voices, *¡Alegría del mar!* Joy of the sea! It was a ritual that belonged to only me and my dad, one of his funny quirks and one of the many moments that made my weekends and summers at the beach so happy and carefree.

Boca Ciega was a small, not very fashionable beach community made up of tiny cottages and a few two-story buildings. A small river flowed through the hills down to the beach and ocean below. The mouth of the river dried up in the summer, which meant we could swim in fresh or salt water. But it also created a swamp that was a breeding ground for mosquitoes the size of pigeons.

My parents, as young lovers, had started camping in Boca Ciega before I was born and rumor had it that I had been conceived in a secluded sea cave. By the time I was eight or nine, we had a small cottage, not much bigger than two rooms, with a kitchen and bath. We had a narrow front porch and a tiny backyard with a lopsided brick barbecue my dad had built himself. The house was painted a brilliant blue, the same color blue used in the Mediterranean to avert the evil eye, and the porch ceiling was a radiant yellow. The living room was red, the bathroom turquoise, and the one bedroom was bright orange. You would have thought it was a Buddhist temple, but none of us had ever been to Tibet or met a Lama—at least not during our current incarnations. People joked about it, but I thought it was beautiful.

All the families on our street had known each other for years and the kids were inseparable. We broke down into age groups, so I belonged to the eight-to-ten-year-old cluster. Our days were very full. Mornings were devoted to sloshing around in the water, not "going out too far." Sometimes Papi would take us on a snorkeling adventure, occasionally spearing an unsuspecting snapper cruising by. When we came home with our catch, Mami would clean the fish and cook it in a very simple sauce for our dinner. In the afternoons when the sun was high we rested, pretending to nap. If the day was overcast, we'd gather beach plums for Doña Cecilia, who ran the *"comedor,"* the common dining room where most families had their meals. Late afternoons, after the heat of the day had dissipated, we took to our bikes and the world was ours. Sometimes we traveled as far down the coast as the next town.

In the early evenings we rode our bikes behind the mosquito truck—spraying was necessary because of the swampy river. The truck bellowed and bilged and created a very real cloud of insecticide, which we followed with great diligence. We knew the truck for what it was—a savage dragon. Our sole and noble purpose was to chase the warlike creature to its cave where, once he let his guard down, we would blind, then kill him, and save the city from his fiery destruction. Our inability to see where we were going, between the flames and the smoke (never mind our coughing), made it all that more exciting.

As the dragon once again escaped us, disappearing over the horizon, and the small truck retired for the evening, we—tired from the battle and nearly drowned by the fumigation vapors—would finally go home. Our moms would be waiting with a shower, a brush, and some harsh words. Every night we'd promised we would never do it again, a promise our moms never really believed and we never really kept. (No one knew then how harmful those fumes actually were.) Only after we had cleaned up, still flush from our triumphs, would we be allowed to accompany our parents over to Doña Cecilia's for dinner.

Even though I was a finicky eater, I truly appreciated Doña Cecilia's cooking. I particularly liked the beach plums in syrup that she cooked in her enormous cauldron or the blue crabs in a spicy sofrito, special dishes to us kids because she had prepared them with ingredients we had gathered. It made us feel important—we were part of something and contributing to everyone's well-being.

After dessert we would catch fireflies or trap more blue crabs for the next day's meal, blinding them with our flashlights. If we were in a quiet mood we would walk on the beach, stepping in and out of the water, kicking to see the phosphorescence created by the millions of microscopic organisms living in the water. It was incredible fun to see the luminescent green whorls that stayed on our skin for a second or two. Magic. Or we'd lie on a grassy dune to count the shooting stars.

This was my magical kingdom. I loved Boca Ciega for the beach itself, for the fun we had riding our bikes and running free. Mostly, though, I loved the beach because it was where we came together as a family, enjoying each other and laughing a lot. In Boca Ciega we became the family of my dreams; no arguments, no scolding, no catch-as-catch-can irregular meal hours with everyone sitting at the table at different times. No, here in Boca Ciega we were the nuclear family, glued together by our common experiences and by love.

Snapper Fillets with Tropical Salsa

In truth, Mami prepared the snapper, be it red, white, or yellow-tail, in many different ways, sometimes grilled, rarely baked—it was too hot to turn on the oven—but most often simply sautéed in butter or olive oil and finished with a squeeze of Key lime. When she was particularly happy she gave it an extra flourish with a little side of salsa. Simple as this recipe is, the most important thing is the freshness of the fish, so buy carefully. Fish should have no odor and be firm to the touch.

4 red or white snapper or yellowtail fillets (5 to 6 ounces each)
½ teaspoon salt
1 tablespoon olive oil
Juice of 2 Key limes

Rinse, dry, and trim the snapper fillets. Sprinkle with salt.

In a heavy nonstick skillet big enough to fit the fillets without crowding, heat the oil to high. Sear the fillets, and once they're browned on both sides, lower the heat to medium and cook until the fish can be flaked with a fork, 2 to 3 minutes on each side. Remove to a warm serving plate and keep warm. Just before serving, squeeze the limes over the fillets. Serve plain or with a flourish of tropical salsa.

Tropical Salsa
1 ripe mango, diced
1 roasted piquillo pepper, minced
½ Habanero chile, seeded and minced

2 shallots, minced
Small pinch of smoky pimentón
½ cup mint leaves, torn into small pieces

Combine all the ingredients in a bowl and let stand for 20 minutes until the flavors meld. Serve the salsa on the side.

Enchilado de Jaibas (Blue Crabs in Sofrito)

It wasn't so much that we loved crabs as it was that we caught them. Some nights the kids would go out (parents in attendance) flashlight in hand to blind the little creatures. There were hordes of them and they clacked and clacked. We imagined them to be the cavalry of a great invading army and we, as defenders, set out to destroy them. It was a team operation—one kid shone the flashlight in the eyes of our scared crab and the other grabbed it from behind and threw it in a sack. Funny how kids in their innocence can be so cruel. I am still ashamed. Nevertheless, this is a great party dish. Just make sure you have plenty of large paper napkins. You can, if you wish, use freshly cooked crabmeat from the fishmonger or even the canned variety, just make sure it is of high quality. Stone crab claws are an excellent substitute as well.

This recipe, like so many others in the Caribbean, starts by saying *"haga un sofrito,"* make a sofrito, a basic preparation of sautéed onions, bell peppers, garlic, tomatoes, the lynchpin of many a dish, but this one is that and more! Serve with white rice to sop up the sauce, and sautéed ripe plantains to counterbalance the spiciness of the dish.

For the Sofrito
3 tablespoons olive oil
2 large onions, minced
1 large red bell pepper, minced
½ green bell pepper, minced
5 garlic cloves, sliced
3 ripe tomatoes, grated

1 tablespoon sun-dried tomato paste
½ cup chopped parsley
1 bay leaf
Salt and freshly ground black pepper to taste
½ teaspoon smoky pimentón
½ teaspoon spicy pimentón
½ cup dry white wine
2 pounds blue crabs, cleaned

In a large casserole heat the oil to medium hot, add the onions and peppers, and sauté until soft. Add the garlic, the grated tomatoes, and tomato paste and stir to dissolve. Reduce at high heat for about 3 minutes. Add the parsley, bay leaf, pimentón, and wine.

When the mixture is bubbling, add the blue crabs, turn the heat down to a simmer, cover, and cook for 5 or 6 minutes. If using cooked crabmeat or stone crab claws, cook until just heated through.

THIRTEEN

Hurricane Carlos

My dad was a *ciclonero,* a kind of storm chaser, who got excited when a hurricane was announced. He enjoyed the *preparaciones,* as we called them, which consisted of buying all the condensed milk the bodega had on hand, crispy Cuban crackers, and tins of sardines. The windows were taped (that was our only protection), and every pot, pan, and bucket came out of hiding to serve in catching leaks. The hurricanes were thrilling. We loved the howling of the wind and even standing in several inches of water. It felt cozy, all of us together, huddling and eating at the same time. Since Don Juan's house was only a lean-to, he'd come over to be with us as soon as the first hurricane warnings were announced. I loved that he let me cuddle with the constantly trembling Joselito.

Once everything had been tended to, Papi would put me in the car (my mother refused to participate) and off we went, just he and I, to the Malecón, the big seawall that surrounds Havana. We parked as close to the seawall as we could and in between furious squalls and storm surges, waited for the huge waves to jump over the car and the occasional fish to hit the windshield.

After the hurricane came the second act. Papi went out to "do good" with me in tow. He drove through fallen trees and looked for anyone who might need help. This too was exciting; still, it was a good lesson by example.

The power would not come back on for a few days. Road signs for gas stations and small businesses blew off, as well as any terrace furniture that had been left out. In Havana there was little damage to the well-built concrete houses or buildings, but there was devastation in Las Llaguas and other shantytowns. Fallen trees were left on the streets until they could be cut in pieces small enough to cart away. There were lots of leaves and branches all around, some flooding and broken glass.

The beaches and the countryside were much more affected than the city. Boats ripped from their moorings, denuded beaches, and flattened small towns with few wooden houses left standing were the norm after a powerful hurricane.

As devastating as the hurricanes could be, we felt content, we were safe, we had each other, and we had condensed milk.

Sardine and Potato Salad

Mami never made this salad except during a hurricane, and as kids we didn't exactly love it, but now I think it's delicious. The trick was "cooking" with no electricity, but we had a gas stove, so it wasn't too bad.

For the Potatoes
2 large Yukon Gold potatoes, peeled and sliced ½ inch thick
2 bay leaves
½ teaspoon sea salt
½ teaspoon freshly ground black pepper
Olive oil for drizzling

For the Salad
4 cups mixed greens, dressed in a vinaigrette
Three 4-ounce cans sardines in olive oil, cut in halves lengthwise
¼ cup capers
Pimento-stuffed olives, sliced
4 hard-boiled eggs sliced
Juice of 1 lemon
Olive oil, preferably good-quality Spanish

For the Vinaigrette
½ teaspoon coarse salt
¼ teaspoon freshly ground black pepper
Juice of 1 small lime
3 tablespoons virgin olive oil
1 teaspoon mayonnaise
½ teaspoon Dijon mustard

Boil the potato slices with the bay leaves and salt until done, 12 to 15 minutes. Sprinkle black pepper. Drain and drizzle olive oil over them.

Arrange the dressed lettuce on a large platter, and pour the vinaigrette on top. Make a bed of potato slices on top of the lettuce, and arrange the sardine halves on top of the potatoes. Sprinkle the capers and sliced olives on top and place the egg slices around the platter. Sprinkle with lemon juice and douse with really good Spanish olive oil.

Dulce de Leche Ice Cream

Of course we had no electricity during a hurricane, no ice to crank in the old ice cream maker, but we did have a gas stove and it was all about the condensed caramelized milk anyway. We spread it on Cuban crackers and gorged on the special treat until we felt sick, but since we were not allowed to eat it until the next hurricane, we took full advantage.

In ice cream form, the *dulce de leche* is even more of a treat to those who didn't grow up with it. (So believes Häagen-Dazs with their successful *Dulce de Leche* ice cream.) For me it is the only way I can justify indulging in condensed milk these days.

For best results, and so as not to tax yourself unnecessarily, break the recipe into steps and make the *dulce de leche* the day before. Refrigerate it until ready to use.

For the Dulce de Leche
1 can condensed whole milk

For the Ice Cream Base
2 cups milk
1 cup heavy cream
1 teaspoon vanilla extract
4 large egg yolks
⅓ cup sugar
1 cup broken pecans

For the Dulce de Leche
To make the dulce, place the unopened can in a heavy pot and completely cover with water. Bring to a boil, then keep at a high

simmer for about 3 hours, making sure the water level is maintained. Allow the can to cool before opening it. Scrape the milk into a bowl, cover, and refrigerate.

For the Ice Cream

Heat the milk and cream in a heavy saucepan over medium heat until bubbles form around the edge. Remove from the heat.

Stir the egg yolks and sugar together in a medium bowl. Pour some of the warm milk and cream mixture into the eggs while stirring. Return this mixture to the saucepan and cook over low heat until it thickens slightly. It should lightly coat the back of a wooden spoon. Add vanilla, stir, and cool completely.

To make the ice cream, pour the milk and egg mixture into an ice cream maker and process according to the manufacturer's directions, but only until it thickens somewhat. While the ice cream is churning, add the *dulce de leche* one-quarter at a time, making sure it is completely integrated before the next one-quarter is added. Add the chopped pecans and churn for a few additional minutes. Transfer to a plastic container and freeze for several hours until firm.

FOURTEEN

The Keeper of the Flame

Every family had one: a tía (aunt) who was the official keeper of the birthday and saint's day flames, graduations, engagements, weddings, the proclaimer and celebrator of all the official and semiofficial dates in the family.

Tía Patria was my mother's eldest sister, the one who gave the wettest kisses, the longest hugs, and to whose home one always went when asked—the one who told you not to cross your legs and that your dress was too short or too tight or simply "inappropriate." She made you kiss your cousins, especially when you were mad at them. She made you sit quietly until you "cooled off," and at every family gathering, she made you listen to the same old story told by the same old uncle who was deaf, from the country, and more than a little boring.

If you were sick, she made and brought chicken soup and didn't leave your side until you were appreciably better. When you visited her, she always made the dishes you liked best and made them the way you liked them. And as good as she was every day, she was simply magnificent when it came to birthdays.

Cuban birthdays were celebrated with fervor. Whether you were a child or adult, the menus were similar. There seemed to be a need to juxtapose sweet with salty tastes, and there was enough variety to satisfy every palate. The *pastas de bocaditos*, sandwich spreads, ranged from elaborate to deceptively simple, but they were all delicious.

There were always *croqueticas*, thimble-size croquettes, *empanaditas*, tiny pastries, *carne fría*, a type of Cuban paté, and at least two types of cake and ice cream, homemade and tropical.

The birthday cakes were simple and very sweet: a basic yellow cake heavy on the sugar and spread with guava marmalade or peach puree and covered in meringue. We were also big on rum and syrup cakes, the heavier and the sweeter the better. But the pièce de resistance was the *brazo gitano*, a jelly roll type of cake known as Gypsy's Arm (page 117).

Bocaditos de Fiesta
(Finger Sandwiches)

Tía Patria made much of the sandwiches, as there was always a great variety of spreads, different types of breads and different cuts: triangles, diamonds, straight, rolled. The one constant was cutting the crust off. As she finished, she would place the tiny sandwiches on a platter, arranging them in a circle to form an attractive display. Then she covered them with a moist linen towel and refrigerated them until ready to serve. The moist towel kept the sandwiches from drying out, so they could be made the day before. Any type of extra thin bread with crust off will do, as well as any shape—round, triangular, strips, or cookie cutters.

The Spreads

Shrimp Triangles
¾ cup chopped cooked and peeled shrimp
1 roasted red bell pepper, well drained
4 pickled cocktail onions
½ cup mayonnaise
1 tablespoon chopped olives
Salt and freshly ground black pepper to taste

Place all the ingredients in a blender and process to make a smooth spread. Adjust the seasoning and spread on extra thin crustless bread. Cut into triangles.

Chorizo Diamonds
3 ounces cream cheese, softened

3 ounces crumbled Spanish chorizo without its skin
½ teaspoon red pepper flakes
¼ cup chicken broth

Place all the ingredients in a blender and process to make a smooth spread. Adjust the seasoning and spread on extra thin whole wheat bread. Cut in diamond shape.

Blue Cheese Circles

4 ounces Cabrales cheese (Spanish blue)
2 ounces cream cheese, softened
5 tablespoons heavy cream
4 dried figs, finely chopped
¼ cup chopped walnuts

Place the Cabrales in a bowl and crumble with a fork. Add the cream cheese and enough cream to soften. Add the figs and walnuts and stir to mix. Spread on extra thin white bread. Cut into circles.

Manchego Cream

This was my favorite—the height of sophistication, I thought, so original, so exquisite. Many years later, I was sad to discover it was not my Tía's invention but only a variation of the classic French Mornay sauce.

1 egg yolk
3 tablespoons unsalted butter
2 tablespoons grated shallots
1 tablespoon all-purpose flour
½ cup scalded whole milk
½ teaspoon Dijon mustard

A few gratings of nutmeg
1 cup grated Manchego cheese

Slightly beat the egg yolk in a bowl and set aside. Melt 2 table-spoons of the butter in a saucepan, add the shallots, and cook until soft. Add the flour and stir. Add the scalded milk while whisking. Add some of this mixture to the egg yolk, mix, and return the egg mixture to the pan. Continue to stir and cook for 2 or 3 minutes.

Add the mustard, nutmeg, and cheese. Stir vigorously until all the cheese is melted and the sauce is completely smooth. Add the remaining butter and stir. Allow to cool somewhat before spreading on extra thin white bread. Cut into squares.

Here Are Some Other Types of Sandwiches Tía Made

- Deviled Ham Spread: Equal parts of deviled ham and cream cheese with a few dashes of hot pepper sauce.
- Olive Spread: 8 ounces cream cheese to 2 ounces pimento-stuffed olives processed together.
- *Piquillo* Spread: Equal parts of cream cheese and canned roasted *piquillo* peppers processed together.

Carne Fría
(Cuban Paté)

Another staple of the birthday party buffet, thinly sliced and served on saltines, the Carne Fría was a family favorite. It's sort of the Cuban version of a country paté, makes a good little *tapa*, and a great sandwich on toasted French bread with mayo. This recipe makes two 9-inch rolls and can be halved successfully.

Yields 30 servings as an appetizer.

½ pound ground beef
½ pound ground pork
½ pound ground ham
¾ cup grated onion
2 grated garlic cloves
½ cup chopped green olives
1 teaspoon black pepper grains
1 teaspoon salt
Pinch of ground cloves
Pinch of allspice
Pinch of nutmeg
2 slices white bread soaked in milk and tightly squeezed
2 eggs, slightly beaten
3 cups chicken broth

Place all the ingredients except the broth in the electric mixer and mix well using the dough hook or the paddle.

Shape the mixture into two 1½-inch rolls and place on a clean kitchen towel or triple strength cheesecloth. Wrap tightly while pushing the meat roll toward you. Tie up the ends with twine.

Place the broth in a pot large enough to accommodate the meat rolls. If necessary, add water to bring the liquid up to the middle of the rolls. Bring gently to a boil, turn down to a medium simmer, and cook for about an hour, turning once.

Remove from the cooking liquid and allow to cool before unwrapping. Wrap in plastic wrap and refrigerate overnight. When ready to serve, cut into thin slices.

Strain the cooking liquid and freeze for a soup or a sauce.

Lobster Croquettes

Don't feel intimidated by the long list of ingredients—the recipe is easy to understand and make if you break it down in steps—and the delicious results are very well worth the trouble. Tía, who had more patience than I, used to make these the size of a thimble.

For the Béchamel

8 tablespoons (1 stick) unsalted butter
¾ cups all-purpose flour
1 teaspoon salt
Freshly ground black pepper to taste
2½ cups hot whole milk
¼ teaspoon red pepper flakes
1 tablespoon seafood essence*
1 ounce grated Manchego cheese

For the Lobster

1 teaspoon unsalted butter
1 cup minced onion
8 ounces cooked lobster meat, coarsely chopped
½ teaspoon red pepper flakes
2 tablespoons minced parsley

For Frying

1 cup all-purpose flour (or more)
1 large egg
2 tablespoons cream or milk
1 cup fine bread crumbs (or more)

Canola oil for frying

*Seafood essence comes in concentrated form and can be found at gourmet markets.

For the Béchamel

In a medium saucepan, heat the butter until it foams. Add the flour, salt and pepper, and red pepper flakes and stir with a whisk. Gradually add the hot milk while stirring. Continue to stir until the sauce thickens and becomes shiny. Add the seafood essence and the cheese and stir to mix well.

For the Lobster

In a small skillet, melt the butter and wilt the onion. Add the cooked lobster and the rest of the ingredients and stir. Add the lobster mixture to the béchamel and stir.

Transfer to a platter and spread evenly. Cover with plastic wrap and refrigerate until completely cool. It is better left overnight.

To Make the Croquettes

Sprinkle flour evenly on a work surface. Beat the egg and cream together in a bowl. Place the bread crumbs in another bowl. To shape the croquettes, dip a teaspoon in oil and use it to scoop up a small amount of the lobster batter and shape it into a small cylinder. Lightly roll it in flour, dip in the egg, and roll in the bread crumbs. Place on a platter until ready to fry. Repeat until the lobster mixture is all used, adding more bread crumbs as necessary. (The recipe can be made ahead up to here.)

To Fry

Place 2 to 3 inches oil in a heavy skillet, preferably cast iron, or in a deep-fryer. These will take a higher temperature. Heat the oil to 375°F over medium-high heat.

Fry the croquettes a few at a time, no more than five or six, moving them with a slotted spoon to make sure they are golden on all sides. Transfer to a platter lined with paper towels and keep warm in a low oven until all are done. Do not cover or they will loose their crunch.

Brazo Gitano with Citrus Cream

I have never understood why this cake is called Gypsy's Arm—it couldn't be less like one! It's a rolled cake, soft, plump, and pale— the opposite of what I think a gypsy's arm looks like, all graceful movements and sinewy forms, arms raised to dance or stretched to play an instrument. But *Brazo Gitano* it is called, and *Brazo Gitano* it shall be. This cake has remained a favorite in the family, perhaps for its exotic name but I am sure for its taste. Once you make it you will understand why.

For the Citrus Cream
Grated zest of 2 oranges (careful not to include any pith)
1½ cups fresh orange juice
1 tablespoon lemon juice
½ cup sugar
4 large eggs, slightly beaten with a pinch of salt
2 teaspoons cornstarch dissolved in 1 tablespoon water

For the Cake
Softened butter for greasing the pan
6 large eggs, separated
Grated zest of 1 orange
Grated zest of 1 lemon
1½ cups confectioners' sugar
½ cup all-purpose flour
¼ cup cornstarch
1 orange, sectioned, for garnish (optional)

For the Citrus Cream

Place the orange and lemon zest, orange juice, and sugar in a saucepan and stir to dissolve the sugar. Add the eggs and stir over low heat until mixture begins to thicken. Add the dissolved cornstarch and continue to cook, stirring until thick. Pour into a bowl, cover, and reserve.

Preheat the oven to 350°F. Cover a jelly roll pan with a large silicone baking mat, or lightly butter the pan, cover with parchment paper, and butter the paper. The paper should cover the sides.

For the Cake

Put the egg yolks and grated zests and lemon juice in an electric mixer and beat for 1 minute, just to mix well. Add 1 cup of the confectioners' sugar and beat until the mixture forms a ribbon and is light in color. Transfer to a large bowl.

Wash and dry the mixing bowl and beat the egg whites with the remaining confectioners' sugar until stiff.

Sift the flour and cornstarch together.

Fold one-third of the meringue and one-third of the flour mixture into the yolk mixture, being careful not to deflate the batter. Repeat.

Pour the batter into the prepared pan and gently spread evenly with a large spatula. Place the cake on the middle rack of the oven and cook for 8 or 10 minutes, just until the batter begins to pull away from the edges. Do not allow the cake to color or it will dry out and crack when rolled.

Wet a linen or cotton kitchen towel and wring dry. Place on the kitchen counter. Immediately after taking the cake out of the oven, turn it onto the towel. Trim the edges of the cake with a sharp serrated knife. Evenly spread the cake with the citrus cream. Using the towel to handle the cake, roll it tightly lengthwise.

Transfer the cake to a serving platter and allow to cool completely. Cover lightly with plastic wrap and refrigerate until firm.

To serve, sprinkle with additional confectioners' sugar, using a strainer or flour sifter. Garnish the platter with orange sections if desired.

Yields 8 to 10 servings.

FIFTEEN

Noche Buena 1949

The last time I saw Santa flying in the Havana sky was Christmas Eve 1949. I was ten but still very innocent. I know now I couldn't have seen him, but see him I did. The image of Santa in full regalia—sleigh, reindeer, and bags of toys—has stayed imprinted on my mind to this day. I had been standing on the balcony waiting for my dad to come home from one of his mysterious outings while my mom played with a snow globe. A Christmas Eve party was going on all around us.

When Papi finally arrived very late, he acted as if nothing was wrong, a look of total innocence on his face and some lame excuse on his lips. Mami chose to ignore him for the sake of the party. It was obvious to her he had been with another woman. But I was ignorant of all that and just happy he was there. Our entire family and the extended cast of characters were there too. Usually we had our big Christmas Eve dinner, Noche Buena at Tía Patria's house, but this year Mami had wanted to do it at home and everyone had come.

The party was in full swing—we were having such a good time. Everyone was laughing and talking and eating. It was wonderful, not only because we were all together as a family, including my favorite aunts and uncles, favorite cousins and both of my brothers, but Pupen and every other being I loved was there too.

And I knew Santa was sure to leave me many, many presents.

Cooking aromas pervaded the house and the kids were eager to eat. But the grownups were still drinking and my cousin José Antonio (my age, ten) got drunk on everybody's leftover drinks. I was sure he was going to get spanked, but he wasn't. Everyone was in a good mood and laughed at his daring. The *lechón*, a whole roast pork, had just been delivered from the bakery's oven (ours wasn't big enough) and it filled our home with the scent of spices and garlic. The intermingled smells of all that was cooking drew us straight to the table.

While we feasted on roast pork and turkey, just emerged from the oven with Mami's special stuffing, as well as roast guinea hen, rice, beans, yucca, *malanga*, plantains, *turrones,* and the very special *Tarta de Santiago,* Mami was making up her mind to leave my father. A few weeks later they separated for good.

That was to be the last Noche Buena I was ever to have with my whole family.

Christmas Turkey with Catalán Stuffing

Since there were so many other things served at the Noche Buena table, Mami always chose a small turkey. I prefer them too. This recipe can be broken down to make over two days; marinate the turkey and prepare all the makings of the stuffing without mixing and keep them in bowls covered with plastic wrap. Both the turkey and the stuffing ingredients need to be refrigerated. As soon as the turkey goes in the oven you can mix the stuffing and place it in an ovenproof container to bake separately.

For the Adobo (marinade)

8 tablespoons (1 stick) melted sweet butter
½ cup light olive oil
4 garlic cloves
Grated zest of 1 orange
1 tablespoon salt
1 teaspoon black peppercorns
1 teaspoon chopped fresh rosemary
1 teaspoon chopped fresh thyme
½ teaspoon ground cumin
½ cup orange juice

For the Turkey

One 10- to 12-pound turkey
1 cinnamon stick
Peel of ½ orange
1 bay leaf
1 small onion spiked with 2 cloves

For the adobo, place all the ingredients in a food processor and pulse until well mixed.

For the turkey, separate the skin from the flesh and season the turkey well with the adobo. Rub the adobo on and under the skin, inside the cavity too. Cover with plastic wrap and refrigerate overnight.

Before roasting, make a little packet of the cinnamon, orange peel, and bay leaf. Place with the onion inside the cavity of the turkey, and truss.

To roast the turkey, preheat the oven to 350°F. The turkey should be cooked for 15 minutes per pound without stuffing as in this recipe.

Place the turkey on a roasting rack in the oven pan. Cover the breast with aluminium foil and keep it covered until the last hour of roasting. Using a baster, baste quickly every 20 to 30 minutes. The turkey is ready when the inside temperature is 180°F or the leg juices run clear.

> Note: Take the turkey out of the refrigerator at least 1 hour before roasting. If you have been baking and the kitchen is very hot, take it out only 30 minutes before placing in the oven.

For the Catalán Stuffing

2 tablespoons olive oil
4 ounces white butifarra,* crumbled
8 ounces honey-baked ham, diced
2 cups freshly toasted bread crumbs
1 cup diced dried apricots

1 cup minced celery

1 large Fuji apple, peeled and diced

8 tablespoons (1 stick) melted butter

¼ cup minced parsley

½ teaspoon ground cinnamon

½ teaspoon ground black pepper

2 cups chicken broth, or more as needed

½ cup dry sherry

*A type of Catalán sausage available in some Latin markets. As a substitute, use sweet Italian sausage or preferably veal sausage.

Heat the oil in a large pan and sauté the crumbled *butifarra*. Add the ham, the bread crumbs, and the rest of the ingredients except for the broth and sherry. Stir well. Cook at medium heat, adding chicken broth and sherry as needed to keep the mixture moist. Transfer to a buttered baking dish.

Wait until the last hour before the turkey is ready to place in the oven and bake for 1 hour and 30 minutes.

Tarta de Santiago (Saint James's Almond Tart)

This classic tart hails from Galicia, in northwest Spain, above Portugal, where my father's ancestors come from, and indeed there is a small city in that area by the name of Carballo. The classic design on the tart is the silhouette of either the scallop shell or the cross associated with Saint James and the pilgrimage to his city.

> *4 large eggs*
> *Pinch of salt*
> *1 cup superfine sugar**
> *1½ cups (about 8 ounces) finely ground toasted almonds***
> *8 tablespoons (1 stick) softened unsalted butter*
> *½ cup freshly ground bread crumbs*
> *Grated zest of 1 lemon (with absolutely no pith)*
> *¼ cup confectioners' sugar*

> * *If superfine sugar is not available, pulverize sugar in the food processor.*

> ** *Pulverize almonds in the food processor, or use almond flour available in gourmet and health food stores.*

Preheat oven to 400°F. Place the eggs in a medium-large bowl and add a pinch of salt. Mix using electric mixer until loose. Add sugar and mix until very fluffy and light yellow, about 4 minutes.

Add ground almonds and mix thoroughly. Add the softened butter and continue to mix. The batter will be fairly loose at this point. Add the fresh bread crumbs and the grated lemon zest, and continue to mix until well blended.

Pour into a tart pan with a removable bottom and place on a baking sheet. Place the baking sheet at the bottom of the oven, not the bottom rack, for exactly 10 minutes or until it begins to color.

Lower the oven's temperature to 375°F and transfer the baking sheet to middle rack. Bake for another 15 minutes or until tart is golden brown. Test by inserting a toothpick; it should come out dry.

Place on a rack to cool. When ready to serve, place a scallop shell over the tart. To make a silhouette of the shell, dust it with confectioners' sugar using a flour sifter or strainer.

3

HAVANA IN THE
FIFTIES

SIXTEEN

The Broken Home

The fifties began with a deafening silence. The raucous chaos of the household was no longer. Nobody seemed to be speaking to anybody except when it was necessary. Tía Berta was not speaking to my mother, my mother wasn't speaking to my father, and all my father did was yell at everyone. Pupen tried, unsuccessfully, to console Mami. Kiki stopped coming every day. Even Don Juan stopped visiting. Dulce lost her touch with fritters and at ten years old I started wetting my bed. Everyone went their own way, no longer being able to find refuge or continuity in each other or in our frenzied daily routine. The family, such as it was, was unraveling.

I knew my parents were going to divorce. They never told me why, but I knew well enough the reason was that my father had "other women" even though, to her credit, Mami never said anything to me. Even much later on when I was fully aware of the reasons for the divorce she never spoke ill of my father to me.

Divorce wasn't so common in the Cuba of the fifties and I couldn't help but feel a certain shame about it. My mother cried a lot and Papi wasn't around most of the time. Almost overnight our household changed from being loud and joyous to one that felt, and indeed was, bereft. The same loving passion my parents had felt for each other was now translated to silent reproaches and palpable anger. I felt completely abandoned and deeply, deeply sad. I didn't want to take an active part in any of it, so I took refuge in Abuela Monona's (my dad's mother) and Tía Berta's room.

Tía Berta was an interesting case. She was a dentist but had abandoned her practice. She had a married son with whom she could have lived, but chose to live with us and look after Abuela. Mostly she kept herself confined to their room, not venturing out for the several-times-a-day ritual *café* or even for meals. Dulce had to knock on her door and leave the coffee or her meal on a small table outside the room. Tía Berta wouldn't take anything directly from Dulce or from my mother. She thought Mami was trying to poison her.

Tía Berta spent the day reading, sometimes out loud to Abuela, and she often mumbled to herself, but their room was quiet and off limits to everyone but me (mostly because Tía felt threatened and thought "someone" was going to cut all her clothes to shreds). She was a schizophrenic, but *our* schizophrenic, who loved me deeply and was very gentle with me. At some point during the process of everything falling apart Tía realized I had not been doing my homework at all and set out to help me. I was still at Ruston Academy just before being sent to Catholic school in Havana. I had never been very studious—curious, yes, but not studious. On the few occasions I did do my homework, I did it on my own; Mami never monitored. My grades improved greatly once Tía Berta started helping me.

Sometimes on Sundays, when Dulce was off and the family out, Tía went into the kitchen and made something special for me. I was not supposed to share it and if she found out I had, she'd storm—and I mean storm, smoke coming out of her ears—into the kitchen and throw out whatever was left of the special treat. With that look of rage in her face, she was not one you would want to disobey.

Abuela was calm and sweet, belying the many years she had made my grandfather Don Pancho, long dead, suffer in silence. She had been quite a beauty in her time, capricious, impulsive, and a spendthrift, but now she was lost in the fog of senility with only moments of lucidity. We teased her by passing ourselves off (with the appropriate disguises) as one distant relative or another, and she was always good for a dollar. She had taken to saving her fried eggs on a plate in the big armoire to give me as an after-school snack. She would also retrieve the flat silver we used every day one piece at a time to hide under her mattress. After all it was hers, the only thing left from the many beautiful objects she had once owned. The silver was important to Mami too if for a different purpose. She would pawn it every time she needed some cash.

Tía and Abuela, these two disparate beings, knew I was undergoing a difficult period and they were trying the best they could to comfort me with kindness and with food. But my soul had already been torn from my heart, and my life would never be the same again.

Tía Berta's Coconut Kisses

I love these not only because they were sweet and a little gooey but also because of their name. Since Tía was not welcome in Dulce's kitchen, she had to wait until Dulce took her afternoon rest to rush in and make a commando raid in the shortest time possible. I was grateful for her kindness—a side of her tormented personality we didn't see very often. She wasn't much of cook either, but these besitos required very little skill and just three ingredients—that much she could handle. I used to nibble on them slowly while doing my homework, and it made studying much easier.

> *1 package (7 ounces) grated sweetened coconut flakes*
> *½ cup condensed milk*
> *1 egg, well beaten*
> *Chocolate syrup for garnish (optional)*

Preheat oven to 300°F. Combine the coconut, condensed milk, and egg in a bowl. Mix well.

Place a silicone baking mat on a cookie sheet or butter the cookie sheet. Using a teaspoon, drop small mounds of the mixture onto the cookie sheet.

Bake for a total of 15 to 18 minutes, until kisses begin to color and are firm but still chewy. Remove from oven and let cool on cookie sheet.

Place on serving dishes and drizzle with chocolate syrup.

Pudín de Pan de Abuela Monona (Abuela Monona's Bread Pudding)

Abuela Monona, my dad's mother, never was much of a cook but there were certain dishes she had always liked to make for her youngest child, my father. This bread pudding is one of those. She could no longer make it herself but on an occasional day of lucidity she directed Tía Berta very precisely.

4 eggs
1 cup sugar
3 cups whole milk
1 cinnamon stick
4 tablespoons melted butter
1 tablespoon dark rum
1 large brioche bread, thinly sliced, or challah (Abuela used sliced media noche buns)
¾ cup toasted almonds

Preheat the oven to 350°F. Cream the eggs and ¾ cup of the sugar until thick. Put the milk and cinnamon stick in a saucepan and bring to a boil, then lower the heat to low. Pour half the milk into the egg mixture and mix well. Return the egg mixture to the milk saucepan and stir constantly until the mixture has thickened slightly and coats the back of a wooden spoon. Remove from the heat and pour the mixture into a bowl. Discard the cinnamon stick. Add the melted butter and rum and stir until well blended.

Butter a baking dish and sprinkle with sugar at the bottom of the dish. Arrange slices of brioche slightly overlapping. Sprinkle some almonds on top of the bread. Pour some custard over the brioche and continue making layers until the brioche, almonds, and custard are all used. Cover with plastic wrap and weight down with a heavy can on a plate. Allow to soak for 30 minutes. Brush the top with the remaining butter and sprinkle with the rest of the sugar.

Bake in the middle rack of the oven for about 45 minutes to 1 hour or until the pudding is golden and puffy. Serve with extra custard or with light sour cream.

SEVENTEEN

The Convent

Other than the snob appeal of boarding school, I was against the idea of being sent away. At fourteen I liked the thought of traveling alone and visiting new places, but the idea of leaving Havana, the parties, and my friends nearly broke my heart. Besides, I had already had two of the most unpleasant years in Catholic boarding school in Havana, during the time my parents were divorcing. I had been sent away so I wouldn't have to live through more wretchedness. When I went home every weekend I had the same realization time and again; boarding school was so much worse than my short stay with our ever so fragile family. In fact, the only good experience I took away from that horrible school was meeting Graziella. Graziella and I met at snacktime over Spanish almond cookies. We recognized an underlying loneliness in each other and saw how those lovely, delicate *polvorones* actually made us feel better.

Now, however, it was for real. I was being sent away to school in the States "to perfect my English and learn some discipline . . . because it would be good for me." I didn't see how. I never liked rules, I wasn't good at taking directions, and having been raised in the Cuban version of a *Noises Off* road show, I was a poor candidate for the confining environment of a convent school.

Before Catholic school in Havana, I had attended Ruston Academy—one of the most liberal and progressive schools in the city—since kindergarten. Unique in its approach to pedagogy, it was co-ed, did not require uniforms, had small classes, individual attention, international faculty, multicultural students, and a system of education that encouraged reasoning and individuality. My teachers tolerated my less than diligent approach to homework because I paid attention in class and participated in all discussions, showing amply that I had indeed learned well the lesson of the day. I was certain I could never expect this kind of treatment in a convent school, especially given the experience I had had with the Dominican nuns, partly because of my disrespect for organized religion.

Not having been brought up a Catholic, even nominally (baptized only because I had asked), I brought serious misgivings to my new stateside school. I knew it was going to be a difficult period; I didn't know so much as the Our Father. We weren't big on prayers at home, and we didn't believe in God's will. My father was more likely to speak of the natural law of cause and effect than to believe a capricious God would want things this way or that, dispensing punishment and grief at will. But against all reason, my parents sent me to a Catholic–convent–boarding school anyway.

I arrived in Mazer, Pennsylvania, after a change of planes in Atlanta, where walking toward the terminal I saw a sign that read "Colored Baths Inside." I thought they meant tiles, colored tiles. "How sweet," I thought. "They want you to have an aesthetic experience." Then some mousy-blond lady in a hat yanked me by the sleeve before I could go inside. Then there was a long train trip from Pittsburgh, plus a forty-five-minute drive to Saint Ignatius Academy.

I was not prepared for the imposing Tudor campus facing me.

Everything about the grounds and buildings was ominous, the turrets, the stone façade. It was as cold inside as it was outside. Bare walls, high ceilings, and a floor so highly polished I could see my reflection. It made me think of a forbidding, faraway castle in the British dunes I had seen in an old black-and-white movie. If the place was meant to scare me into compliance, it nearly did. I felt my soul leave my body. To make matters worse, after a brief settling in, I realized I would be required to make my own bed, do my own laundry, and spout dogma. What circle of hell had I been delivered into?

I quickly earned the nickname of Doubting Thomas and was expressly forbidden to ask questions in catechism class or spend time in the library. The only saving grace, which spared what little dignity I had left, was my friendship with Claudia and the occasional weekend spent with her family. Mrs. Miller, Claudia's mother, was so kind to me that one Thanksgiving, forgoing the classic American turkey, she prepared a pork roast for dinner just because she had heard that Cubans love pork. In addition to the traditional trimmings she made, I made some parslied potatoes and helped with a luscious pumpkin soup.

At school, I was always late for meals. Sister Miriam, who made us pray for Senator Joe McCarthy every day, would sometimes make everyone wait to sit down and say grace until I came into the dining room, all eyes (I swear some of them evil) upon me. It was meant to embarrass me, but I thought it was funny. I was never in a hurry to face the flavorless food we were served. The only thing I liked from the school menu was a soupy stew of meat and potatoes that, once doctored with ketchup and pepper, reminded me of the Cuban *carne con papas*.

I wasn't allowed to take art or join the drama club until my algebra grades improved. They never did, so I didn't learn to draw or act and the world was spared a tortured artist and another drama queen. I got detention for reading a Gandhi biography instead of the *Life of the Saints,* which Sister Teresa had assigned to me.

As director of the choir, Sister Agatha would only allow me to mouth the words of the hymns lest I throw everybody off. She may have had a point—I still can't carry a tune. But I thought, I'm singing my little heart out in (fake) praise of the Lord, don't I have a right to be heard? I bet that if Jesus wanted to, if it made a difference to him, he would make my voice just as sweet as my classmates Nancy's. That alone was proof to me that Jesus was neither divine nor was there a God.

The rolling of my eyes at prayers and my missing the evening rosary so often prompted sweet, tiny Sister Josephine to talk to me about my faith. "You have to pray for faith, my dear." Which I thought was a ridiculous statement—to pray for faith you first have to have faith in faith! And on and on we would go in circles.

But she was kind to me, Sister Josephine, despairing at my inability to believe and fearful for the fate of my soul. Every once in a while she would sneak me a brownie that Sister Angeline baked to celebrate one of the nun's birthdays. Sister Josephine would give me hers, sacrificing her modest pleasure for mine. That small act of compassion did more for the state of my spirit than anything else in the miserable years I spent at that school.

Sopa de Calabaza (Caribbean Pumpkin Soup)

2 tablespoons olive oil
2 shallots, chopped
½ carrot, chopped
2 pounds calabaza (Caribbean pumpkin), peeled and diced
4 cups chicken broth
Salt to taste
Freshly ground black pepper to taste
½ cup half-and-half
½ cup chicken broth
Minced parsley for garnish (optional)

Heat the oil in a casserole, add the shallots and carrot, and sauté briefly. Add the calabaza, stir, and cover with the chicken broth. Bring to a boil, reduce the heat to medium, add pepper and cook covered for about 30 minutes or until the vegetables are tender.

Transfer to a food processor and blend to make a smooth soup. Return the soup to the stove, add the half-and-half and stir until heated through. Taste and add salt if necessary. If you feel like gilding the lily, transfer to a warm tureen and sprinkle with minced parsley.

Asado de Cerdo con Repollo y Manzanas (Pork Roast with Red Cabbage and Apples)

Mrs. Miller made this pork roast or something very similar for Thanksgiving dinner. I thought it was the most original dish and the best thing I ever ate. It wasn't until many years later I learned to make this Nordic classic in cooking school. The traditional cut to use is the loin, but since pork nowadays is lean to the point of mean, I use pork shoulder.

> 2 to 3 tablespoons canola oil
> 3 to 4 pounds pork shoulder
> Salt and freshly ground black pepper to taste
> 1 medium onion, sliced
> 1 small head red cabbage, cut into thin slices
> 2 Gala or Fuji apples, sliced
> 1 heaping tablespoon sugar
> Bouquet garni (½ rib celery, 2 bay leaves, several sprigs parsley tied together)
> ¾ cup red wine

Heat the oil in a Dutch oven or a large heavy casserole. Generously salt and pepper the pork and brown well on all sides. Remove from the pot.

Add the onion and cabbage and stir to mix. Add the apple slices and sprinkle with sugar. Return the pork to the pot and nestle it into the vegetables. Add the red wine and bouquet garni.

Cover and cook at a simmer for 1 hour and 45 minutes to 2 hours, turning once at the halfway point of the cooking time. Continue cooking until very tender and the internal temperature reaches 160°F.

Discard the bouquet garni. Remove the roast from the pot. Allow it to rest about 10 minutes before carving into thick slices. Place the cabbage and apple at the bottom of a warm serving platter and overlap the slices over the cabbage. Deglaze the pot with a little hot water, scraping up all the brown bits, and pour all the cooking juices over the pork.

EIGHTEEN

My Brother Clive and the Attack of La Varicela

In 1955, when I was sixteen, after two and a half unbearable years of Catholic boarding school in the States I came home for Christmas. A few days before I was scheduled to return, Clive gave me an unexpected present: *varicela* (a type of measles). He was in his first year at the Air Force Academy and had caught it from one of his classmates. We were both too old for this *varicela*, which we should have had as children, but I was delighted to have been infected, since it meant delaying my return to school by at least another week.

Clive and I were in pretty bad shape. We itched and picked at our *ñañaras* (a much more amusing word that pustule), playing up the discomfort for all it was worth. Mami put us in the same room to contain the contagion, but principally to minimize her trips to our bedsides. We were constantly asking for one thing or another, far exceeding her motherly patience and annoying each other as well. Aubrey, my other brother, went unscathed but claimed spoiling rights just the same. Mami tried to calm us down by cooking soothing dishes like a *malanga* mash (Cuban penicillin) and preparing soft-boiled eggs just the way we liked them.

By the time Clive and I had recovered, I had missed so much school Saint Ignatius Academy wouldn't take me back. Poor *moi*, I had to stay in Havana. I was thrilled!

Puré de Malanga y Boniato (Malanga and Boniato Mash)

Malanga, in any of its forms, is mother's milk to Cubans. A touch of *boniato,* another prized tuber, makes this puree even better. It has a rich, deep flavor and earthy tones. Since both tubers are very starchy, they need a lot of liquid.

1½ pounds malanga
½ pound boniato
2 teaspoons salt
3 tablespoons butter
½ to ¾ cup hot whole milk

Peel the *malanga* and *boniato* and cut in small pieces, then place in a heavy casserole and cover with ample water. Add the salt. Bring to a boil, lower the heat, and cook for about 30 minutes. Discard the water, drain well, and pass the tubers through a ricer or vegetable mill back into the casserole. (Do not use a food processor because the high starch content of the tubers will change the texture and make it unpleasant.) Add the butter and stir. Continue to stir while slowly adding the hot milk until achieving the desired texture.

Huevito Pasado por Agua (Soft-Boiled Eggs)

Our soft-boiled egg was more a rite than a recipe. For one thing, it had to be called *"huevito,"* the diminutive for egg. Then it had to be cooked exactly 3 minutes from the time the water boiled. It had to be served in a *café con leche* cup warmed in hot water, not a bowl. (Bowls were too big and the egg would get cold.) First went a pat of butter, then one crumbled cracker, not saltines but the really crunchy type from the El Carmelo bakery (no other would do). More butter, the carefully cooked egg, a bit of salt, more butter, and another half (exactly half) crumbled cracker. Clive got two eggs because he was a man.

Ponche de Leche para los Enfermitos (Milk Punch)

I loved this drink. It was a special treat to have when we were sick or had a cold, and I didn't mind being one or the other or both if it meant I could have punch. During our *varicela* experience when Clive felt well enough to go into the kitchen, he prepared a *ponche de leche* for us. His with dark rum, mine with a teaspoon of port. By now I was having such a good time, I nearly forgot I had to return to boarding school when I was well.

Boil a cup of milk, take the pot off the stove, and air and foam the milk with a soup ladle at least three times. Place in a bowl beat an egg yolk with as much sugar as you like, until the sugar has lost all its graininess and the yolk has lightened in color. Add rum or port wine to taste and stir. Slowly pour the milk in and stir. To make more froth, pour from one glass to another at least twice, keeping one glass about 8 inches higher than the other. Serve.

NINETEEN
Where the Boys Were

I came back from the States to live with my mother in an apartment provided for us by my Tío Trampo, who had assumed responsibility for us after my parents' divorce. My father had remarried and had a step-daughter a little younger than I. He was living in the same house where we had lived as a family. I resented everything about it. I suspected his new wife had been one of the "other women" and the girl, even if she wasn't, liked to say that she was my father's daughter. The magical relationship my father and I had shared now changed from loving to explosive; we slammed doors, hung up on each other. It was an intense relationship—we were wary of each other, and acted like star-crossed lovers. He was always late picking me up and naturally that deepened my sense of abandonment. I was very jealous of his new family. I was also profoundly sad and troubled.

This situation, coupled with my experience in convent school, made me eager to rejoin the ranks of the frivolous and cheery. Boys, of course, were an integral part of the fun. I reconnected with friends, principally Graziella, my friend from grade school and al-mond cookies. She was very active socially and knew all that was going on in our very limited horizon of school, competitive sports, and beach clubs. Graziella knew who was going with whom, who was available, who had been seen holding hands, who had won the last swimming meet, and most important, who was going to have the next party. Crucial information in the life of a person who by now was seventeen years old.

Graziella and I belonged to the same beach club. My membership and charging privileges came only through the good graces of my Tío Trampo. My dad thought "the club" was pretentious. My mom thought it was harmless. It was innocent enough fun: swimming, sailing, flirting, and attending parties. And it was fertile ground for boyfriends. There was Eddy, who didn't know I existed, and the mild-mannered Emeterio, who I briefly considered marrying for his family's wealth and a way out of my present circumstances. Rafael, who was three or four years older, was desperately in love with me, but I felt uncomfortable around him. He was handsome and nice enough, but I recognized in him "traits" similar to Tía Berta's, and sure enough, he ended up in a psychiatric hospital some years later. It was all right to have odd boyfriends, even somewhat strange boyfriends, but truly loony ones were another thing altogether.

Then there was the elusive Moisés. He and I liked each other a lot. I was seventeen and he was almost nineteen. For that alone Mami wasn't fond of him. But love has its ways and we managed to sneak to the movies alone several times and have endless conversations in the boathouse at the club, where we thought no one could see us. Nevertheless, his mother found out. When she realized our perfectly innocent secret relationship had been going on for a few short weeks she was adamant that Moisés not see me anymore. I couldn't understand why until Moisés pointed out I wasn't Jewish, but then I understood even less. Blame my dad, or blame Ruston Academy, but I just could not see what difference it made. We had to stop dating completely, but we still managed to speak on the phone, all the more eagerly now that all contact was forbidden. Mrs. Montoro found out, of course, and as a result Moisés was simply not allowed to use the phone.

Several weeks of longing went by until one day at the club Moisés approached me with an invitation from his mother to a special occasion dinner, Passover. She would call my mother herself to reiterate the invitation. I understood it to be a very big deal.

Moisés came to pick me up in a car with a driver and a rather formal air. We were to be at his home by late afternoon before sundown. After we arrived and the introductions to his parents and sisters were made, we sat in the living room pretending to make conversation. I felt very uncomfortable. Lots of delicious nibbles were passed around, including some almost red, hard-boiled eggs with a faint taste of onions, *huevos haminados,* which Rebeca, one of Moisés's sisters, explained were cooked for hours and hours in water and onion peels. The delicious eggs were a double respite, as a treat and for allowing us a break from having to talk.

We were called to the table, where two candles stood unlit in their very ornate holders. Mrs. Montoro covered her head with a shawl, lit the candles, and said some prayers. I had never seen this done and I thought it was both beautiful and touching.

The food started coming, the likes of which I had not seen or tasted before. I was intrigued by everything, the more so because Moisés explained the significance of the foods and the rituals throughout the meal. At some point everyone started singing at the same time. I must have looked bewildered because Moisés immediately launched into an explanation about the Four Questions and how Sephardic Jews had ways and rules different from the Ashkenazi. Since all I knew about Judaism at the time was that Jewish people did not believe that Christ was divine (a non-belief which seemed reasonable to me), I was totally and absolutely confused about there being two types of Judaism and two types of celebration, even two types of celebratory food.

It was a long but fascinating dinner. I was tired but elated by the many new dishes I had tasted. I was baffled by Moisés's explanations. But mostly I was sad because I had understood very clearly what Mrs. Montoro had tried to do and accomplished so brilliantly. She sent me home alone in the car with the driver. When Moisés tried to accompany me she held him back. That was the last time I saw or spoke to him.

Baked Sole with Avgolemono Sauce

For the Sole

1 pound sole (4 fillets)
Salt and freshly ground black pepper to taste
2 tablespoons unsalted butter

For the Lemon Sauce

5 egg yolks
Juice of 2 lemons
1 cup chicken broth

Preheat the oven to 450°F. Rinse and dry the fillets and sprinkle with salt and pepper. Grease a baking dish with 1 tablespoon of the butter and place the fillets in the dish without overlapping. Dot with the remaining butter. Bake for about 6 minutes or until the fish flakes when tested with a fork.

While the sole is baking, make the lemon sauce. Beat together the egg yolks and lemon juice in a bowl. Heat the chicken broth in a saucepan until just about to boil. Pour some hot stock into the eggs and whisk vigorously. Add the egg mixture to the broth on the stove and whisk together until sauce begins to thicken. Remove the sole from the oven and place the fillets on a warm platter. Pour 2 tablespoons of the cooking juices into the lemon sauce and whisk. Spoon the sauce over the fillets.

Leg of Lamb

In central Turkey this combination of spices is commonly used to season lamb, often with yogurt added to the sauce.

For the Marinade

3 tablespoons olive oil

1 cup grated onion

5 garlic cloves, pressed or minced

2 tablespoons tomato paste

2 teaspoons dried mint

1 teaspoon dried oregano

1 teaspoon dried thyme

1 teaspoon ground cumin

½ teaspoon pimentón picante or hot paprika

1 teaspoon salt

1 teaspoon freshly ground black pepper

3½-pound boned leg of lamb, trimmed and tied

1½ cups chicken stock

Mix all the marinade ingredients together to make a paste. Rub the lamb with the paste, cover, and refrigerate overnight.

Remove the lamb from the fridge about an hour before baking and place in a Dutch oven. Preheat the oven to 450°F. Bake the lamb uncovered for 30 minutes. Turn down the oven to 350°F. Pour the broth into the Dutch oven. Cover and bake, basting every 20 minutes, for 1 additional hour. This braised lamb is best eaten medium-well or well done. Check the internal temperature with an instant thermometer and cover again. Continue to check the temperature every 15 minutes until it reaches 155°F degrees for medium or 160°F degrees for well done.

Remove from the oven. Make a loose tent with foil to cover the lamb and allow to rest for 15 minutes. The temperature will rise another 5 degrees. Untie and slice thinly. Serve with the cooking juices.

Bimuelos

Buñuelos, a corruption of *bimuelos,* have come to mean in Spanish pretty much any sweet fritter. In Cuba the *buñuelos* come in a figure eight and in one version they are made with a combination of yuca, *malanga,* and sometimes *calabaza* kneaded into a dough. In another popular form the *buñuelos* are made out of a dough of flour, eggs, and water. Both types are fried in lots of oil and served with a simple syrup, preferably with a hint of anise. Mrs. Montoro followed the Sephardic preference (common in the Mediterranean basin) for round fritters and in this case made them with matzo meal because of dietary laws.

For the Dough
1 cup milk
1 tablespoon unsalted butter
Grated zest of 1 lemon
3 eggs
Pinch of salt
2 cups matzo meal

For the Syrup
3 cups honey
¼ cup rose water

For Frying
1½ cups vegetable oil mixed with ½ cup olive oil

For the Topping
¾ cup pistachios, finely chopped

Using a large saucepan, bring the milk, butter, and zest to a boil. Remove from the stove and allow to cool slightly.

Beat the eggs in a bowl until well mixed. Add about one-quarter of the milk to the eggs and mix well. Add salt. Return to the milk on the stove and stir vigorously while adding enough matzo meal to make a thick, malleable dough. Transfer to the bowl. Make small balls no bigger than a quarter in circumference. Place them on waxed paper until all the dough has been used.

To make the syrup, bring the honey, rose water, and 1 cup water to a boil in a small saucepan. Reduce the heat to a simmer, and cook for about 5 minutes.

Preheat the oven to 400°F. Heat the frying oil to 375°F in a deep skillet and add the fritters one by one, making sure not to crowd. Moving the oil around with a slotted spoon, fry until golden on all sides. Place the fritters on a cookie sheet. When they are all done, bake in the oven for 5 to 7 minutes to cook through. (Not a traditional method, but it works.)

Using tongs or a long fork, dip each fritter in the honey syrup, transfer to a warm serving platter, and sprinkle liberally with the chopped pistachios.

Makes about 3 dozen delicious fritters.

TWENTY
Under the Stars

My first *enamorado* after Moisés was Emeterio (Eme for short). He was my first almost serious boyfriend. His family were cattle ranchers and immediately objected to me because I came from no money (my father's family fortune was long gone when he was still a young man), I wasn't Catholic enough, and I seemed a little flighty—right on all counts. I wouldn't make a very docile wife. Right again. My mother objected to Eme because she knew I could never be happy on a farm or in the company of conservatives. Everyone seemed to know me all too well and was ready to predict disaster. I really didn't care. It wasn't so much I was interested in their money—I just wanted out of my circumstances: no proper home, facing a very diminished social status, and the fact that I would probably have to go to work.

Eme was very handsome and a little shy, twenty to my almost eighteen, and although we were mad for each other and wanted very much to make love, we never found the opportunity. We dated for several months but were always heavily chaperoned, most often by his sisters, who I am sure suspected my lustful intentions and economic motives. They were determined to save Eme from my greedy little clutches, so they took every opportunity to put me down.

Knowing full well what my father did for a living they would

ask, "What profession does your father practice? I always forget."
"Ah, yes, he is the astrologer Profesor Carbell, but how come
your name is Carballo?" Their snotty attitude annoyed me beyond reason. Who the hell were they, these *guajiritas* still
wrapped in *hojas de tamal?* (country girls wrapped in corn husks).
I was never good at hiding my emotions and the more irritated I
got, the more they taunted me.

Eme's sisters lorded their money over me, and I had nothing
but contempt for them. Our hostility was overt. They didn't read,
they didn't even like to dance—not the most auspicious of circumstances for a cordial relationship. Besides, what parents
would name their daughters María Concepción (conception) and
María Dolores (suffering)?

But the physical attraction between Eme and me was strong
and we kept seeing each other. For New Year's Eve 1957, Eme invited me to *esperar el año* at the Tropicana nightclub with a group
of other young couples. The required chaperones would be present, but we knew there were plenty of dark corners offering the
prospect of kissing in secret.

This was to be a very special evening. Spending New Year's
Eve together was already a big deal, but adding the Tropicana—
that was very important. I had only been twice before, but Tropicana was my favorite of all the big nightclubs because of its
improbability. It was a place that seemed to have sprung quite literally from a pipe dream. It was a flamboyant, decadent, and
truly splendid place.

In Havana, nightclubs and casinos were open every night of
the year. Headliner entertainers from all over the world came to
perform in Havana nightclubs: Nat King Cole, the Cab Calloway
Orchestra (my parents had all their records), Dorothy Lamour,
Edith Piaf, Tony Martin, Xavier Cugat, Carmen Miranda, and the
best of the best Cuban orchestras as well as local musicians and

singers: Rita Montaner, Bola de Nieve, Ernesto Lecuona, and the indisputable king of all that was cool, Beny Moré.

There were plenty of nightclubs to choose from. The Casino Parisien at the Hotel Nacional was the newest. It had dining, dancing, and shows, but the casino part was more important; it was a place for high rollers. It had no attraction for me with its reputation of being an elegant and sober place. Anathema for young and racy Cubans!

The Sans Souci was located in a colonial-style villa that had been renovated and expanded to house gaming rooms and a large stage. The shows mostly featured name acts from abroad.

Montmartre was the most sophisticated of the clubs with its subtle Frenchified airs and very "continental" shows with lush music and refined dancing. The only club to be completely indoors, it was right at the center of Vedado, an affluent residential neighborhood. This had been my parents' favorite of the places they used to go to late in the evening after I was asleep and the household had finally quieted down. They would have a light supper, watch the show, gamble a little, and dance. They loved to dance.

The Hotel Riviera and the Habana Hilton also provided gambling and shows and there were many, many lesser clubs, cocktail lounges with great acts, and bars not considered proper for young women to visit. Those were the places I liked best. Quite different from Tropicana, they were more real, more Cuban, and infinitely more fun with their tinge of danger.

An area of the city known as La Playita was home to the El Pennsylvania and El Panchín among others. Good orchestras played those clubs and the dancing on the floor was frequently hotter than in the shows, more and more uninhibited as the rum flowed and the evening wore on. La Campana was also totally disreputable, with its fist fights and patrons who openly smoking marijuana. It was probably not a fit environment for a young lady.

The one place not to miss was the Ali Bar, where the great Beny Moré and his orchestra became regulars in 1956. Beny would cancel lucrative parties and radio or television appearances to come groove with his musicians. He embodied everything Cuban. He was suave and raucous at the same time. He loved life and he lived it fast. His joy was palpable. He was a charismatic performer, *tiene angel,* we would say, a combination of soul and charisma.

In the center of the old part of the city, along the very wide sidewalks of El Prado, practically facing the Capitol and the Residential Palace, were numerous outdoor cafés. There were still some all-girl orchestras that had been very popular at one time. (That had been one of my childhood fantasies—playing the trumpet in one of these bands.) It was a hoot to sit, sip your drink, and watch the world go by.

Sloppy Joe's, El Floridita, La Bodeguita del Medio were places with character and individuality. It wasn't just a question of décor or even of clientele. Their feel was different. These were places that made you comfortable and relaxed. There was a feeling of the familiar. You didn't have to dress to the hilt or even have a reason or special occasion to stop by. A casual drink on your way to someplace else, or a chat with friends and a lovely cigar were reason enough. And among jaunty hats, two-tone shoes, and locals comfortable in their own skins, were tourists who thought they were doing something naughty.

The electrifying energy of the city was a force unto itself. Havana bewitched with its physical beauty and its enormous charm, leaving one defenseless against its pull. The fabulous clubs, the myriad lounges and bars, the variety of restaurants, and the confluence of the best orchestras that ever played popular music, the shows, the acts, the lounge singers (some sleazier than others) made for an extraordinary nightlife.

But the jewel in the crown, and the most extraordinary of all, was the Tropicana. So it followed that for New Year's Eve at Tropicana, I had to have a new dress, new undergarments, and new shoes. A manicure, pedicure, and beauty salon hair were all *absolutamente necesarios.* Mami wouldn't hear of it, any of it. She wanted me to wear a dress I had worn once to Sans Souci. But I was adamant. I needed a new ensemble. I didn't want Eme's sisters to have more ammunition for their criticism.

I complained to my cousin Lourdes, who told my Tío Trampo, who asked my mother to take me to the seamstress for a new New Year's Eve outfit. The shoes, my first high heels, came from El Encanto, the most elegant store in Havana, considered one of the best in the world. Medium high heels, black gros grain with a satin band on the instep, they were a thing of beauty, the first and only pair of Christian Dior shoes I ever had. They were charged to my uncle, as were a matching set of bra and panties, the same color of my dress to provide confidence with their elegance.

My dress was exquisite. Smoke gray silk faille in a princess cut embroidered with bead work from the shoulders to below the waist. Mami designed the dress to flatter my petite frame, make my shoulders look broader and my chest fuller (not easy do to). My Tía Dora embroidered a paisley design on the dress using bugle and seed beads and the very occasional sequin, following my mother's instructions. Mami had not wanted, nor was she able to afford, another new dress for me, but once the expense was taken care of she was enthusiastic and particular. And she had impeccable taste.

When the day came, I had my hair in rollers for about twelve hours. I did my own manicure, pushed back cuticles and buffed my nails. Mami thought cutting the cuticle was just short of self-mutilation (my ears had not been pierced) and that red nail polish was vulgar. By eight o'clock I was ready. My makeup, carefully applied, was minimal; a little powder, light lipstick, and a little Vaseline on my eyebrows and eyelashes. I would have looked ridiculous in the full battle paint of an artificially drawn mouth and heavy eyebrows that were in vogue.

Mami had taught me how to perfume myself: spray into the air, walk into it, and place a few drops at the pulses and behind the ears. She was allowing me to wear her Guerlain L'Heure Bleue for the first time. All Cuban girls wore cologne as children; it was part of the impeccable toilette, and *the* favorite was Violetas Rusas. At fifteen, I had graduated to Shalimar. Now I had advanced to a heavier, more adult perfume. It seems silly now, but at the time this was an important rite of passage. I finally slipped my dress on, Mami zipped me, and I looked in the mirror. I was pleased.

Girls started their grooming early. Our mothers would take us along to the beauty parlor, where we got manicures mostly with buffed nails, and the occasional light nail polish. We got regular haircuts at the salon, and some of us had our hair done for birthdays and such. As teenagers we were taught how to apply makeup (light, and age appropriate), shave our legs, and always look well groomed. This was part of the training of good and pleasant wives; when your husband came home from work you had to be *"arregladita,"* showered, combed, made up, and perfumed. We also learned how to do household chores—not so much to have to do them ourselves but to be able to direct a housekeeper to do them properly. We, Mami and I, hadn't bothered much with this part, since Mami hated chores and had delegated them to Kiki and Dulce in the past. Now she didn't care much one way or another whether I learned them or not.

Eme arrived in a chauffered car, black, polished to glisten, accompanied by his *lovely* sisters and his *gracious* mother. But we were determined to have a good time and were not going to let anything or anyone spoil it. By the time we reached Tropicana I was too excited to eat very much; *Cuba libres* were the way to go, or the sweet *Doncellitas*. Not too many, that would have been indecorous—one, two at the most, throughout the night.

The Tropicana looked glorious. The gambling room, with its chandeliers and overwrought décor, was right off the lobby. The clientele was elegant and polite, both tourists and locals, but underneath that glossy façade you could feel the feverish excitement that consumes gamblers. Past the *roulette* and *chemin de fer* tables were the nightclub's two dining and dancing areas as well as the semicircular stage, the scene of extravagant shows. The shows often included Santería elements for the benefit of the tourists, and lots of flashy dancing by the principals. Orchestras alternated to do continuous sets so there would be not a moment without music or dancing.

The two areas of the nightclub were quite distinct: one outdoors, with tall trees hanging over the tables, the other indoors but giving the impression it was *al aire libre*, in the open air. A magnificent series of concrete arches of different heights connected only by glass plates covered the indoor floor. The arches seemed to float without support and you could see the stars through the glass. The chorus girls danced on the catwalks that ran among the trees.

Fifty of the most voluptuous and beautiful girls made up the chorus line. The costumes consisted of various shiny, colorful bits of material placed on strategic places, and the tallest, most outrageous headdresses. How those girls could dance on those arches was a feat of engineering. Another of my childhood fantasies had been to grow up to be a *corista* in Tropicana. Those gorgeous *mulata* girls were the Cuban standard of voluptuous beauty. I didn't look anything like that.

After the usual over-the-top floor show, choreographed and

overproduced with exquisite tackiness, Eme signaled me to leave the table. In order to ditch the chaperones, we had previously arranged to meet at a designated dark corner for some unsupervised smooching. As I was walking toward our destination, I leaned down to pick up an evening bag from the floor but Eme, now a few feet behind me, cried out to me not to do it. He didn't have to explain—I knew exactly what he meant.

Small terrorist acts, planted bombs or dynamite explosions, had been happening all around the city. Fidel Castro had been in the Sierra Maestra in Oriente province since early 1956 waging a guerrilla war against the Batista government. Although we were very aware of the events, battles fought in the mountains were all a little too far from the Havana glitz to have much of an impact on the city. So the revolution was brought to us. Small bombs were being planted by Castro sympathizers in stores, movie houses, cafés, everywhere in Havana. The bombs usually didn't do very much damage, but they delivered a message of fear. There was clear defiance as *¡Batista asesino!* graffiti painted in red proclaiming Batista as an assassin appeared overnight on more and more walls.

But neither Emeterio nor I was particularly concerned with politics that night; all we could think of was kissing. We were behind some large palm fronds when we heard an explosion, the unmistakable and very familiar sound of a bomb. There was immediate panic, people running in different directions. The house lights turned bright and the music stopped. We froze. Let them find us being wayward rather than being dead. We didn't know if this was the only bomb or just the first of several planted. We waited a few minutes before going back to our table. We didn't sit down, we didn't speak, everyone was standing up ready to leave. Later we heard a girl had lost an arm. It was rumored the bomb had gone off when she was planting it. Another rumor was that an innocent bystander had picked up the evening bag. I never heard any details, and I'm not sure it was even in the papers. It was a dramatic end to the year 1956.

The incident at Tropicana sobered us enough to start thinking seriously about Eme's and my relationship. Were we on the marriage track or was this just a delicious flirtation? Soon enough, tired of listening to his sisters criticize me and tired of our bickering, Eme broke up with me. He had begun to think that maybe María Concepción and María Dolores were right. I wasn't devastated by the breakup, but I was miffed I had not broken up with him first.

My pride was hurt further when I read the announcement of his engagement in the society pages just a few weeks later. The girl, who I knew only by sight, had been a classmate of María Concepción at El Sagrado Corazón, the most conservative of all Catholic schools in Havana. She embodied what they wanted in a sister-in-law. A very plain girl (fidelity insurance), her father had a gabillion heads of cattle, she was proper, obedient, and had very possibly pledged to stay a virgin till the day she died (even after marriage).

Doncellita

Doncellita means maiden, and this sweet, innocent-tasting drink was supposed to incline us toward our downfall: In a liqueur glass pour 2 ounces cold crème de cacao, then pour 2 ounces cold heavy cream slowly down the side of the glass so the cream floats on top. Garnish with a cherry. How obvious!

Cuba Libre

Place 4 ice cubes in a tall, narrow glass. Pour one measure of rum (or more if you like it charged), dark or light as you prefer, slowly over the ice. Pour enough ice-cold Coca-Cola to fill the glass by three-quarters and squeeze some lime juice in it.

TWENTY-ONE

My Gangster

The Hotel Nacional was the most beautiful hotel in Havana, elegant and luxurious in the classic style. Built on a hill across the Malecón, it was an impressive and imposing sight. Its towers could be seen at a distance all over the city and, in turn, the hotel commanded a view of almost all of Havana. It was a popular spot with both locals and tourists. I often went there with my friend Begonia *"a tomar el sol"*—to sunbathe. We would sit by the morning pool to enjoy the view and ocean breezes, never mind the trouble we would be in if found out. We played the classic shell game with our mothers. My mom thought I was at Begonia's being chaperoned by her mother and Begonia's mother thought we were at the club watching the swimming meets. As we applied suntan lotion, Begonia and I would play at being American tourists, ordering gin and tonics or daiquirís from the bar and *media noches* to nibble on. We thought we were very worldly, but I doubt we fooled anyone.

It was during one of our escapades at the Nacional that I first met Jake, 100 percent American, 100 percent Jewish. He approached Begonia, but she, prettier and ever cooler than I, just tossed her hair and looked into the distance. I looked up and smiled at him. Without hesitation, this short stocky man with piercing blue eyes and thinning hair asked me, "Do you come here often?" Honest to God. He must have been at least twenty years older than I, and I was a few weeks short of my eighteenth birthday.

He told us he was just back from New York, where he had seen *My Fair Lady* on Broadway. I pretended to be impressed and just like that he invited me to lunch. Begonia decided she had had enough sun and left.

Lunch it was and nothing happened. We talked. I liked him. He wanted to know all about me. I was flattered by the attention. We carried on like this for several weeks. In between, he took frequent trips to Miami he claimed were for business. He often brought me back small presents but I would never accept them— it was unladylike to accept anything from a man unless he was a relative or your fiancé. My manners quickly disappeared when he started bringing me L.P. records. It would have taken enormous fortitude to refuse a Frank Sinatra album, especially one with Sinatra's autograph on the cover.

I had to lie to my mother about the provenance of this and the many other albums Jake gave me, and while I had never been much good at lies, I took immense pleasure in lying to her about Jake. I was really getting away with something. She had no idea and would have had a fit had she known. Of course, the secrecy and danger of being discovered made Jake all the more appealing.

Jake would take me driving around Havana in his powder-blue, finned Cadillac convertible—the classic *cola 'e pato*—the status symbol of the fifties. I thought being with an older man, even if he wasn't handsome, was the height of sophistication. Jake liked to spend money, and I was flattered he wanted to spend it on me. He took me to the grown-up restaurants and bars my parents had frequented—recognition of my maturity I was sure, even if we only went for lunch. I loved Sloppy Joe's—it was very informal but was mostly frequented by tourists, a detriment in my eyes. My favorite was Bodeguita del Medio, where we always had roast pork and plantain mash—a really good combination I had loved as a child. It brought to mind maybe I wasn't as mature as I thought, at least not in my tastes.

Whenever we ran into any of Jake's acquaintances, he introduced me as his interpreter to explain why we were together (as it seemed a "nice" girl with an older man was quite scandalous except to me). What Jake did for a living mystified me. He didn't seem to have a job, since he was free all day and he certainly didn't look like a trust fund baby. After much prodding, he finally told me he was a professional gambler. I didn't quite believe him.

But maybe I suspected all along—the money, the Cadillac, Sinatra, I knew it had to mean he was involved with gambling in a deeper and more "personal" way. I took him to be a gangster—*my* gangster. I was thrilled.

A few years before, in 1952, Batista had invited Meyer Lansky, the notorious gangster mastermind, to run the gambling operation in Havana. With his administrative skills, the help of Santo Trafficante, and generous payoffs to Batista himself, Lansky was able to gain control of all sanctioned gambling for the mob. Under his supervision, Havana became one of the biggest international drug ports, and corruption reached unprecedented depths. A lot to say for a country built on graft.

I was vaguely aware of Lansky's dealings and figured Jake was one of Lansky's men—the fact that he was Jewish and I had met him in Lansky territory (Lansky was majority partner in the Nacional's casino) really left no question. I never asked. One afternoon at El Floridita he introduced me to two "pals" of his, Moe and Moe, as very close associates of Mr. Lansky. Were they really notorious or was he kidding? They kept laughing. I didn't know what to make of the introduction, but it made me a little uneasy—that and the fact that Ernest Hemingway was sitting two stools over giving me the once over.

All my dates with Jake took place during the day, since it was impossible for me to get out at night without a chaperone. Finally one time when my mother was out of town, I managed to escape and meet him after dark. (Little did I know that my mother was on a mission to the Sierra Maestra carrying medicines and small arms—but that is truly a whole other story.) Jake took me for a drive, a very long drive, past the lights of the city onto a one-lane road with empty fields on either side.

Back seat, how predictable.

After two or three months of a similar routine, and occasional visits to his hotel, he had moved out of the Nacional and was now living at the Riviera, another swanky Lansky property. I began to feel very blasé about my gangster boyfriend. I was glad to have lost my virginity, but I had never been happy with routine no matter how unusual it might have been. I was beginning to think about breaking up with Jake when one Monday morning he called (he rarely did) to tell me he was going to Miami and would be back in a day or two, as usual. But by the end of the week, he hadn't returned. I had instructions never to call him, so after about ten days I went to the Riviera looking for him. One of the managers brusquely informed me that Jake had checked out and was not returning. And no, he had left no word, no letter, nothing for me. *"No, señorita, nada."*

I tried not to cry, but when I got home, I swallowed a handful of Benadryls. I knew perfectly well that the Benadryls wouldn't kill me, but if I couldn't die, at least I would sleep for a good long while. I told my mother I had a migraine. She knew something was wrong, but she didn't pry. A few weeks later, when I was already over Jake, I received a postcard from him postmarked Las Vegas. On the front was a picture of the Dunes Hotel's ninety-foot pool. On the back, "Wish you were here." There was no return address and no signature.

Daiquirí

2 ounces white rum
1 teaspoon superfine sugar
Juice of 2 Key limes (strained of seeds)

Put the rum, sugar, and lime juice in a cocktail shaker with crushed ice. Shake vigorously but not for long. Strain into a cold martini glass. Or process all the ingredients together in a blender to obtain a frozen daiquirí.

Mojito

The secret to a good mojito, and one few bars use, is mulling the *hierba buena*, a type of spearmint, with sugar, the old-fashioned way, with a mortar and pestle. Then you transfer this mixture to a tall glass and add lime juice, rum, ice cubes, and soda water. I like to add a small piece of the lime zest to mull together with the sugar and spearmint. I think it gives it more of a kick. Many connoisseurs claim there is a legend behind the mojito. Some people attribute the origin of the drink to British pirates. Others claim that slaves received sugared water and rum as part of their daily food portion and so an early version of the drink was born. There was sure to be a rum and sugar drink dating back to colonial times, no doubt, but the mojito in its present incarnation didn't come into vogue until the thirties or forties in the glamorous Havana of the time. The mojito's provenance is of little consequence—what matters is its staying power.

> *6 fresh spearmint leaves and 1 sprig for garnish*
> *2 teaspoons sugar*
> *1-inch piece lime zest (optional)*
> *Juice of ½ lime*
> *2 ounces dry white rum, preferably Bacardi Carta Blanca*
> *Cracked ice (not crushed)*
> *6 ounces seltzer or club soda*

Put the mint leaves, sugar, and lime zest in a mortar and crush well with the pestle. Transfer to a tall glass, add the lime juice and rum and stir. Add the cracked ice and pour seltzer in the glass. Stir, garnish with the mint sprig, and serve. (You can also just mull the sugar and spearmint in a tall glass with a wooden spoon and proceed the same way.)   *Serves 1.*

Paleta de Puerco Asada (Roast Pork Shoulder)

Never far from pork in some form or another, the seasoning in this recipe echoes the flavors of the classic whole roast pig. For Christmas, small families opt for a fresh ham (the hind legs), but it is best made with the fattier shoulder.

One 4- to 5-pound pork shoulder
1 medium onion, very thinly sliced
1 head garlic (peeled)
2 tablespoons dried oregano
2 teaspoons cumin seeds
2 teaspoons salt
1 teaspoon black peppercorns
2 bay leaves
1 tablespoon lard or oil
Grated zest and juice of 1 orange
Grated zest and juice of 1 lemon
Juice of 1 bitter orange (naranja agria)

Using a sharp knife, make several shallow cuts in the pork. Spread the onion slices on the bottom of a noncorrosive roasting pan.

Place the rest of the ingredients in a processor or blender and process to make a paste. Rub the paste all over the pork, making sure it goes into the cuts. Place the pork on top of the onions.

Cover with plastic wrap and refrigerate fat side down for about 4 hours. Turn once and leave the fat side up.

Take out of the fridge 1 hour before roasting. Preheat the oven to 450°F. Place the pork on the middle rack of the oven. After 30 minutes turn down the temperature to 325°F and cook for an additional 2 hours, basting the pork every 30 minutes or so with its own juices. Cook for 30 minutes per pound total, or until the juices run clear and the internal temperature reaches 165°F.

Remove the pork from the oven and allow to rest for 15 minutes before carving.

Fufú de Plátano (Plantain Mash)

This plantain concoction is known as *fufú* in Cuba, *mangú* in the Dominican Republic, and *mofongo* in Puerto Rico. In the Dominican Republic they go as far as having a restaurant dedicated solely to the *mofongo*: El Palacio del Mofongo. Sometimes known as *machuquillo*, in truth, it is equally popular in all of the Spanish-speaking islands of the Caribbean. *Mofongo* is a dish that originated in Africa, where it is still made with sweet potatoes and other tuber vegetables. Once the vegetable is cooked, it is pounded in a large mortar until it becomes a soft puree.

I prefer to mix in the greenness of the plantains; the semiripe ones add a softer texture and a hint of sweetness. I like to serve *fufú* to accompany any meat cooked in a sauce, as it's a great sopper-up.

1 very green plantain (unpeeled)
2 yellow plantains, with no black spots (unpeeled)
6 garlic cloves
Salt to taste
1½ cups pork cracklings (store-bought)
¼ cup vegetable oil

Cut the plantains in 4 pieces each and boil unpeeled in salted water until very soft. It will take about 30 minutes or more.

In a food processor or blender, process the garlic cloves and salt together to make a paste. Using a large knife, cut the pork cracklings into smaller pieces. Set aside.

Peel the plantains and pass them through a ricer or food mill into a bowl. Do not use a food processor, as the mixture will seize because of the high starch content. Blend in the garlic and salt paste. Add the cracklings, then add the oil little by little while stirring. The texture should be that of a thick puree. Work quickly to maintain the heat. Serve at once.

A Note on Plantains

As much a staple as potatoes, plantains are eaten at all stages of ripeness. Each provides a different taste and texture, from deep green *(verde)*, which is very hard and starchier than potatoes, to yellow *(pintón)*, firm yet ripe, to brown black *(manduro)*, which has an aromatic sweetness very much like bananas.

TWENTY-TWO

Roberto, the Man I Married

It was inevitable that I would marry young. I had a strong sex drive, and I wanted to be in control and have my own household. The problem, of course, was my lack of viable prospects. Jake had left Havana and Eme's family had rejected me for being too much myself. I was barely nineteen and I was desperate; all my girlfriends had already married. Graziella was the first at barely seventeen. Her father had wanted to make sure she left home a virgin. No kidding.

Dating, such as it was, really had more to do with the intention of dating—long telephone calls, accidental meetings at the movies, schemes to see each other—than actual, formal courting (visits to the home, scrutiny by the brothers, and sanctioned, chaperoned outings). At nineteen, in 1958, the only way out of my mother's house was to find a husband. And I had no prospects in sight.

Then I met Roberto, or more to the point, Roberto made himself known to me. He followed me out of my cousin's building, where one of his good friends lived. He followed me on the bus. He followed me on the street. He really wanted to meet me but couldn't approach me—it wasn't done. He had to wait until we were introduced. So he found a common acquaintance and arranged for us to meet accidentally at El Carmelo, a popular spot for the *merienda*, the *de riguer* afternoon snack.

Over a *helados tostado*—a mini baked Alaska, a Carmelo specialty—and a *capitolio*, a sort of chocolate cupcake with a heavy swirl of meringue on top, our eyes met and I was immediately smitten. Roberto was a grown man, unlike the boys I had dated (with the exception of my brief *incursion* into the *demi-monde*). At twenty-eight, and with two jobs, he was capable of living independently and supporting a wife, a most desirable quality.

I was impressed with Roberto. A card-carrying intellectual, he was an associate or assistant professor (I never got it right) of philosophy at the Universidad de La Habana and wrote for one of the weekly newsmagazines. He moved in a circle of writers, critics, cineastes, and poets.

One of Roberto's best friends was Guillermo Cabrera Infante, a respected film critic to become famous for his first novel, *Tres Tristes Tigres*. I enjoyed listening to Roberto, Guillermo, and their friends talk politics, literature, and philosophy. Their good-natured sparring reminded me of the stimulating environment of my childhood, listening to grown-ups discuss ideas, abstract possibilities, and what to make for dinner.

Secretly I also enjoyed that Roberto disliked everything American, including my education. He loved foreign films, classical music, and Jean-Paul Sartre. I had heard of Sartre. I admired him, not so much for his philosophy but for his living arrangement with Simone de Beauvoir—lovers, same building, different flats. Roberto loved France and spoke perfect French although he had never been there. I thought it was all very romantic and began to fall in love with love.

It amused me that he hated the heat and complained bitterly about having been born in the tropics. He smoked Gitanes, dressed in dark colors, and favored turtlenecks, longing for the cold days and long nights of another latitude. He thought he looked like Louis Jordan. He didn't. (I thought I resembled Grace Kelly—I didn't.) He thought of himself as an existentialist and quoted Nietzsche and Kant; I had no idea what any of it meant. No matter, I had found another misfit. To my English, he had French. To his Paris, I had Greenwich Village. To his Sartre, I had Kerouac. But for him, I would learn French cooking if I had to.

Before Roberto asked me out formally (our meetings no longer a coincidence), he let me know very seriously that he did not endure chaperones. That could have been the end, but my mother agreed to his conditions, imposing certain limits, mainly no late nights. It was quite special when Roberto arrived to pick me up at home for the first time. I was a little shaken when he said he had chosen the lobby bar at the Riviera Hotel so we could watch the sun set on the ocean. Roberto did not know that the Riviera had been Jake's last residence; Roberto didn't know Jake existed. It was just a coincidence.

As soon as we stepped into the lobby we were escorted to a table by the big plate glass windows. Roberto had specifically reserved it for a better, more romantic view. Without taking his eyes off me he spoke to the waiter, ordering for both of us as was the proper etiquette of the time. The waiter brought two oddly shaped glasses containing silver strainers filled with perfectly slivered ice. He slowly, sensuously poured a brilliant peridot-green liquid over the ice, which magically transformed into an opaque yellowish potion right before my eyes. I'd never seen anything like that. The liquid smelled like licorice and tasted sharp. My first pastis. Would life with Roberto be filled with such discoveries and excitement?

Three weeks later, on our third or forth date, Roberto took me to the Ali Bar to see the legendary Beny Moré, one of the greatest of great Cuban entertainers. Roberto didn't dance, reluctant Cuban that he was, but he knew I loved the music.

Considered by many to be indisputably the greatest Cuban vocalist that ever was, Beny Moré was a romantic balladeer and no one could sing *boleros* like him. He was just as great in anything else. No one ever surpassed him belting out *guarachas, rumbas, sones,* or other high energy numbers. Celebrated for his musicality, he couldn't read music yet he created all the arrangements for his orchestra by humming the different parts of each instrument to the musician playing it. He directed his band with a cane and his body movements. A shoulder thrust forward in the direction of the wind instruments, a fluttering hand toward the piano, a wink, or one of his big smiles was all that was needed. He conceived his orchestra after the big bands of the forties, making many innovations, among them the sheer size of the orchestra—forty musicians—and the introduction of the trombone in Cuban music. He was a musician's musician and a man's man.

El bárbaro del ritmo, as he was affectionately called, was tall and thin, and played to his build. He wore a very personal version of a zoot suit, so original that his pants had a name, *bataola,* which I always took to be (more than likely erroneously) a combination of the words *"bata"* for a girl's dress and the word *"ola"* for wave—his pants literally undulated. From his belt hung a long thick chain that held a watch he kept in his pants' pocket. His jackets went down to his knees and were always at least two sizes too big for his frame. He wore very narrow ties often tied in a bow and he was known for his taste in two-toned shoes. He had style, the icon of all things cool. His records are still being sold today, and there is not one Cuban worth his black beans whose eyes don't water at hearing the first few bars of any of his songs. Beny embodied the Havana of the fifties.

From then on my relationship with Roberto moved pretty

fast. One sweaty afternoon, we tumbled under the sheets and before we could put our clothes back on, I had set a wedding date. In the morality of the day, having sex with your boyfriend (unless he was a gangster) was akin to getting an engagement ring. Roberto knew what he was doing. We had gone to his friend's apartment for this sole purpose.

As soon as we announced our intentions everyone was opposed to the marriage. Roberto's friends because I was an intellectual lightweight, my friends because Roberto was not a member of our club—literally. How shallow could we be? My mother and my father thought I was too young and immature, and after two divorces each, didn't have much faith in marriage. They were adamant that I should not marry at nineteen. However, their deeper concern was that while Roberto looked white, his mother was a *mulata*, light skinned, but a *mulata* nonetheless.

Their argument was not so much a matter of prejudice but of preventing heartache. What if we had children? It was well and good if the children were fair, but what if they weren't? Or worse, what if one was fair and the other had dark skin? This would create serious problems and they wanted to spare me. There were many black professionals, sports figures, and entertainers comfortable in the middle class, but Cuba was not a color-blind society in the fifties. The higher up you went in society, the stronger the prejudice. Being blond or having light-colored eyes was the standard of beauty.

The more my parents refused to give their consent, the more I wanted to marry Roberto. I was considered a minor and, until twenty-one years of age, was required to have my parents' notarized authorization of the marriage. I told them that if they did not give their permission I would move in with Roberto with or without the formality of a piece of paper. I left them no choice but to approve.

Cuban Bouillabaisse

When is a bouillabaisse not a bouillabaisse? Roberto and I never had a real bouillabaisse so to speak, as in authentic from Marseilles made with Mediterranean fish. Never mind, Roberto started calling the fish soup in my *repertoire* by its French moniker and I kind of liked the idea. It was much more elegant than just plain *sopa de pescado* and after all, we did add a touch of sophistication with the pastis (as commemoration of our drink at the Riviera) and the hot pepper sauce, my version of the classic *rouille*. There are a lot of ingredients, but the soup is really very easy to make, since it can be broken down in stages. The only thing to remember is not to overcook it. It is truly worth doing. Read the recipe completely before starting. It makes it easier if you set out all your ingredients before you begin. Read the recipe completely before starting.

For the Rouille
1 roasted piquillo pepper, canned or bottled
1 teaspoon hot pimentón
2 large garlic cloves, pressed or minced
1 tablespoon mayonnaise

For the Fish Stock
¼ cup extra virgin olive oil
1 large onion, chopped
½ red bell pepper, chopped
Fish bones
1 large fish head
2 garlic cloves, smashed

½ teaspoon saffron, toasted and powdered*
1 rib celery, chopped
1 cup thinly sliced fennel
Zest of 1 orange
Shrimp peels (reserved from the soup ingredients)
3 large tomatoes, grated
Several sprigs fresh parsley
Sea salt

For the Soup
1½ pounds red snapper fillets, cut into pieces
¾ pound squid, cut into rings
½ pound medium shrimp, peeled (reserve peels for the fish stock)
8 large diver scallops
Sea salt and freshly ground pepper to taste
1 torn bay leaf
Large pinch thyme
Large pinch oregano
¼ teaspoon saffron, toasted and powdered*
2 tablespoons olive oil
½ cup pastis
½ cup orange juice

*To toast saffron, place a large pinch of saffron threads in a skillet over medium heat until dry. Do not use any oil or butter. Place the toasted threads in some aluminum foil and press with the back of a spoon.

To Finish the Soup
A few strands of saffron
Slices of French bread dried in a slow oven (not toasted) and rubbed with garlic

For the rouille, blend all the ingredients together in a blender or food processor. Transfer to a bowl and reserve.

For the fish stock
Pour the oil into a large casserole and sauté the onion and bell pepper until wilted. Add the bones, fish head, and shrimp peels and sauté for a few minutes. Add the rest of the broth ingredients and stir to coat, then add 12 cups water. Bring to a quick boil, lower the temperature, and simmer for about 30 minutes. Strain well and discard all bones. Return the fish stock to the casserole.

For the soup
Place all the fish, squid, shrimp, and scallops on a platter or a cookie sheet. Sprinkle with salt and pepper, the torn bay leaf, the thyme, oregano, and powdered saffron. Add the olive oil and half the pastis. Rub with your hands to coat all the pieces well.

Bring the stock to a boil and add the orange juice and the remaining pastis. Slip the fish in and cook for about 3 minutes. Add the shrimp and squid and cook for 2 minutes, and then add the scallops. Stir and remove from the heat. Cover and allow to rest for about 5 minutes.

Before serving add a few strands of saffron, just for the beauty of it, and stir. Maybe add a little more pastis or more saffron to taste. To serve, place a slice of bread at the bottom of each individual bowl. Distribute the fish and seafood evenly on top of the bread, adding a ladleful of soup on top of that. Accompany with the rouille for everyone to take a little to dissolve in their soup.

Capitolios

After several failed efforts to recreate El Carmelo's *capitolios* I took the easy and deliciously simple way out: Duncan Hines's divine brownies with walnuts to which I added some more chopped walnuts. The original *capitolios* did not have any nuts in them but in my bastardized version I think they add an appropriate textural interest. So there.

For the Capitolio Brownies
1 box (17.6 oz) Duncan Hines Chocolate Lovers Walnut Brownies
1 cup roughly chopped walnuts

For the Meringue
½ cup corn syrup
¾ cup egg whites, approximately 6 large egg whites
¼ cup sugar

Prepare the brownie mix according to the package instructions. Stir in the additional walnuts and pour into buttered cupcake molds. Bake according to the instructions. Remove from the oven, unmold the cupcakes, and cool on a rack.

To make the meringue, heat the corn syrup to the boiling point. Remove from the heat and set aside. Using an electric mixer, beat the egg whites until they form soft peaks. Add the sugar and beat the whites to stiff peaks. Gradually add the hot syrup while continuing to beat the egg whites. This will make a firmer meringue.

Place the meringue in a pastry bag fitted with a ½-inch tip. Start piping the meringue on the brownie cupcake from the outside rim in, building diminishing circles on top of each other to form a spiral. The smallest meringue circle ends in a peak. You can toast the meringue with a torch if you like, but that is not traditional either.

TWENTY-THREE

Preparing for Married Life

To help us set up house before our wedding, Mami bought us four wrought iron chairs and a small round French-bistro-style table, which she placed under a striped interior awning she had had installed. We could drink our pastis or our *café au lait* (certainly not the Cuban *café con leche*), and Roberto could indulge his Parisian café fantasies. We also managed a chest of drawers and a fairly new sofa. Roberto bought the bed, my aunts and cousins came up with the necessary kitchen paraphernalia, and that was that.

My real preparation for marriage was a crash course in housekeeping and cooking from my mother's cousin América (named after my grandmother). This was no girlie game anymore, and there was no pretending I knew how to iron or how to cook. The funny thing was that having grown up around such wonderful cooks I had never felt the need to cook myself. I was afraid of failure, of course. There was something else: neither Tía Patria nor Dulce liked "other people" in their kitchens and if they gave you a chore, like peeling vegetables or picking beans, you were relegated to the dining room table. But this was for real. I had challenged myself to learn to cook, so experts were called in. My future mother-in-law was consulted for food preferences; my cousin Coqui, married for two years, for ease of preparation; and finally my mother's cousin América, not only considered the best cook of her generation but also the thriftiest and best organized, came to do battle.

Armed with a notebook and pencil, I went to my first lesson. América began with a discourse on when, where, and how to buy. She followed her instruction with field trips. She took me to the butcher shop to show me the different cuts of meat appropriate for different dishes and to the poultry shop for how to choose a live chicken and what to look for: clarity of eye, plumpness of breast, firmness of feather. You made your choice, handed it over to the *pollero,* continued on to other errands, and came back for a bird plucked, cleaned, and cut to your specifications. I still shudder!

Then it was the fishmonger and on to the produce stands, mostly run by Chinese who grew the vegetables themselves. She knew exactly what color, texture, and smell everything should have and what was a fair price to pay. There was a friendly familiarity between América and the merchants in her neighborhood, and this graciousness was also an important part of the exercise.

The most valuable lesson I learned from América was menu planning. Out came the trusted notebook. First we made a list of main courses, then we thought of accompaniments. We placed them in a sort of order that would not repeat the same dish twice in a row. Then we would study the plan, figuring out how to make more than one meal from any one particular dish in order to use the leftovers creatively.

Roast chicken for lunch meant chicken salad—or *croquetas* for the following day's supper. *Carne asada,* Cuban pot roast one day, meant beef sandwiches the next.

The last task after we planned the menu for the week was to

make the shopping list and determine which day we had to shop for what item. At that time in Havana it was customary to shop for dry goods and pulses once or twice a month and to shop daily or at least three times a week for produce and meats.

The typical Cuban meal was not very exciting, often consisting of rice and beans in one or another incarnation, plantains or a different tuber vegetable, and a variation of meats or fish. Pork chops, thin and marinated, were fried and would be accompanied by *congrí,* white rice and red beans cooked together and served with a good portion of fried ripe plantains. Practically everything was fried, and there was always rice. We ate a lot of pulses in heavy stews, a legacy from Spanish immigration, stewy meats and chicken like *carne con papas* and *pollito en cazuela,* and rice, always rice. In fact, the measure of a cook was taken by how good her plain white rice was.

The heaviest meal was taken at lunch at home followed by a short rest or a siesta and the evening meal was something light, an omelet or soup, a sandwich, maybe just *café con leche* and toast.

América taught me first to shop and then little by little how to cook Cuban. She even taught me how to make salads (not too popular in most Cuban kitchens). It was all good basic training and a great foundation for all that other fancy stuff I learned at le Cordon Bleu years later.

Ensalada de Rábanos Rallados (Grated Radish Salad)

Roberto always liked salads (this is considered a peculiarity among Cubans). He was not only fond of different lettuces but loved the crunch and spicy bite of radishes, especially with a strong dressing.

For the Dressing
½ teaspoon coarse salt
¼ teaspoon freshly ground black pepper
Juice of 1 small lime
3 tablespoons virgin olive oil
1 teaspoon mayonnaise
½ teaspoon Dijon mustard

For the Salad
4 large radishes (2 red and 2 white, just for the fun of it), trimmed
1 medium carrot, trimmed
½ Vidalia onion, very thinly sliced
4 small handfuls mixed spring lettuces

In a wooden bowl whisk together the components of the dressing.

On the coarser side of the grater shred the radishes and carrot right into the dressing. Add the sliced onion and toss with your hands. Refrigerate for about 30 minutes before adding the lettuces, then toss again.

Avocado and Red Onion Salad

Nothing could be simpler, even for a newlywed, than this salad. The secret is to find the avocados in their prime. You could, if you wish, add diced tomatoes or sliced hearts of palm or both, but why mess with perfection.

2 Hass avocados
½ red onion, very thinly sliced
Juice of 1½ limes (I like it sharp)
¼ cup extra virgin olive oil
Salt

Peel and slice the avocados and place on a serving plate. Distribute the onion slices evenly over the avocado. Squeeze the lime over the salad and literally douse the salad with really, really good olive oil. Sprinkle with salt. Don't even think about the calories, especially as you sop up the leftover oil with some excellent French bread.

Country Flan

This flan recipe was Cousin América's mother's, who brought it to Havana from Manzanillo in Oriente province, where she was born. It is very much in the Cuban taste, using both condensed and evaporated milk. It is easy to make and it soon became a favorite of Roberto's along with Pupen's coconut flan.

For the Caramel
1 cup sugar

For the Flan
One 11-ounce can condensed milk
One 13-ounce can evaporated milk
4 eggs
1 teaspoon vanilla extract

Preheat the oven to 325°F.

To make the caramel, put the sugar and ¼ cup water in a heavy saucepan and stir to combine. Bring to a boil and watch very carefully until it becomes a light golden caramel. Do not stir, or the sugar will crystallize. Pour into a paté mold, a 10 x 4 x 3-inch mold, or a round 5 cup capacity mold and tip from side to side to cover the bottom and sides well. Set aside.

To make the flan, put the condensed milk, evaporated milk, eggs, and vanilla in a food processor and mix or stir the ingredients together by hand. Be sure they are well mixed. Pour into the caramelized mold. Place the mold in a larger pan and carefully add boiling water (this is a hot water bath) to come a third to halfway up the sides. Bake for 1 hour and 15 minutes. Remove the mold from the oven and then from the water bath, let cool briefly, then refrigerate. Do not unmold until completely cold. Loosen the edges with a thin knife blade and place the bottom of the pan in some hot water, very briefly. Place the serving plate on top of the mold and invert to unmold. Serve.

TWENTY-FOUR

Le Marriage

Cuban women of my generation married young, and I was the last to do so in my group of friends. We usually married someone a bit older who had finished his education and was working and therefore able to establish a separate household. By and large, we were a frivolous group of young women who did not take studying too seriously. Our mission was to marry, have children, and run the household.

Fathers didn't like long engagements, as these put virginity at risk. But planning for a wedding was taken quite seriously. Most girls had a large wedding and it took the better part of a year to sort out the details. Guest lists required the most intricate of negotiations, although almost everyone the parents, bride, and groom knew would get an invitation. Even those who didn't have a large reception still had a big church wedding.

Since Roberto and I were not much on convention, our wedding was a nonevent. My father did not have the means to give me a big wedding, but I really did not want one either. It seemed absurd to me to spend so much money on a party, and neither Roberto nor I was a practicing Catholic. Besides, none of our friends, his or mine, was particularly happy about our impending marriage. I wasn't even too sure myself.

We were married December 12, 1958, by a Notario Público. I

wore an empire dress, a light knit indigo blue, with a V neck and a flat bow at the center. Roberto looked handsome in his dark gray suit. In attendance were Roberto's mother and my mom and dad, who had brought me a purple orchid corsage. It was meant to be worn in the center of my chest, but unmindful of my father's feelings, I found it "too tacky" to sport. Our two witnesses were Guillermito Cabrera Infante and another friend of Roberto's.

After we signed the papers, we all went for a bite and a drink at a nearby popular restaurant. Before Roberto and I had finished our sandwiches, we left the group to go to the movies. We had not wanted to miss a single minute of the new German film playing at our neighborhood theater. That was our honeymoon.

Roberto took a few days off, but we were too broke to travel anywhere. We didn't mind. At all. We spent the time going to the movies, going out to dinner, getting used to one another, and engaging in the traditional honeymoon pursuits. I thought it was all so grown up and sophisticated.

To my surprise, I was eager to try my hand at domesticity. I had always liked the thought of cooking and now all I had to do was follow Cousin América's advice. My time with her had paid off. I had my notes and without hesitation I just started to cook.

Classic Cuban a la Carballo

Some years ago it already took five counter men at 60 hours a week each, plus a slicer—a young man whose only job is to prepare and slice the 1,820 pounds of ham, 1,680 pounds of roast pork, and 1,200 pounds of Swiss cheese—and five gallons of pickles and 2,100 loaves of Cuban bread, to keep the patrons of the Latin American Cafeteria on Coral Way (in Miami) in Cuban sandwiches for one week. The place mostly serves *especiales*—one-pound sandwiches that are a large meal by themselves. Mine is a somewhat more modest take on the sandwich and I also use prime ingredients and French bread—Cuban bread in the States tastes like cotton. NO MAYO!

6-inch length of French bread
1 teaspoon mustard, preferably Dijon
2 ounces honey-baked ham, thinly sliced
2 ounces roast pork, thinly sliced
2 ounces sliced Swiss cheese
4 thin pickle slices
1 teaspoon melted butter

Slice the bread lengthwise. Pull out a little of the doughy part and discard. Spread the bread with mustard. Layer on the ham, pork, cheese, and pickles; press the sandwich together and brush with melted butter. Place in a panini press, cook for about 2 minutes, just enough to crisp the outside and slightly soften the cheese. If you don't have such a panini press, put the sandwich in a skillet and weight it down with another heavy skillet. Heat the sandwich briefly on each side. Slice in half at a pronounced angle and serve.

Makes 1 sandwich.

For the Media Noche Version

The *media noche* differs from the Cuban sandwich only in the bread used. It is made with an elongated, slightly sweet, and very soft egg bun, which can be purchased at Cuban markets or bakeries.

TWENTY-FIVE

December 31, 1958: The Revolution at our Door

New Year's Eve 1958, Roberto and I decided to stay home and have a quiet dinner so I could show off my new cooking skills with a Catalán stew (it may not have been hot, but it was still winter) and mango shortcakes, do the honors with champagne cocktails, play at being urbane, and go to bed before midnight to show our lack of respect for the holiday and the government.

It was no sacrifice, no one felt like celebrating. The mood was somber and the streets empty. The tension was palpable.

Terrorism continued to escalate and in retaliation, there were more and more political murders, gun battles, and torture. Batista took great pride that his army mutilated his opponents and, as a further deterrent, would show their bodies on television.

Popular sympathy was with Fidel Castro. Fidel was a charismatic figure; his professed passion for justice lived in all of us. Most important, he had promised to return the country to a democratic republic as soon as elections could be held. Anyone who had a social conscience was very well aware of the injustices toward the rural population and the abuses of power under Batista. Even though there was a large middle class of professionals, technicians, and business owners, there was also great dichotomy between the very rich and the very poor. We were well aware change was needed and it was in that vein we supported Fidel's proclaimed ideals of fairness, equality, and opposition to the corruption and oppression of Batista's government.

Political violence and rampant corruption were part of our heritage. In Cuba anything could be bought or sold, anything or anyone. Since the time Cuba became a republic in 1902 to the last gasp of the Batista government, members of the government *du jour* became rich overnight. It was a putrid environment.

Nevertheless in 1958, Cuba was experiencing unprecedented prosperity, the standard of living was high even for the middle class. We were an advanced country by world standards with an enviable expansion in education and health care. Infant mortality was the thirteenth lowest in the world and illiteracy rates were around only 17 percent.

The annual budget for the country was $400 million a year, with a favorable trade balance; Cuba was solvent, reporting astonishing economic growth. The population had doubled in less than sixty years. Our standard of living was the highest in the Americas only behind the United States and Canada, and higher than many European countries. There was a doctor for every 980 inhabitants, a car for every 27, a telephone for every 28, a refrigerator for every 19, a television set for every 10. There were 600 movie theaters, 58 newspapers, and 126 magazines. In workers' wages, Cuba came fourth, behind only the United States, Canada, and England. In gold reserves and assets, Cuba held third place in the Americas. Our social legislation was the best in all of the Americas only second to that of the United States. Nevertheless, prosperity didn't assure security—it was too unstable an environment for that.

Now those two explosive worlds, prosperity and social injustice, were colliding at our door.

Champagne Cocktail

1 lump sugar
2 dashes bitters
Chilled champagne
1 twist lemon peel

Place the sugar lump in a chilled champagne flute. Add the bitters and fill the flute with chilled champagne. Add the lemon twist and serve.

Catalán Stew

A distant cousin of my mother's who had been living in Spain for several years sent her this recipe by mail. It's a standard recipe easily found in any Catalán cookbook but at the time we were enthralled with the idea that it called for chocolate in a meat dish, a novelty in Havana. It also calls for a cinnamon stick, which is just as magical here as in the *Pollito en Cazuela* on page 214.

1 tablespoon olive oil
2 ounces thick-cut bacon, diced
Salt and freshly ground black pepper to taste
2 pounds very thin lamb chops
1 large onion, chopped
6 garlic cloves, sliced
1 heaping tablespoon flour
¼ cup medium dry sherry
1 cup beef broth
1 bay leaf
1 sprig fresh rosemary
1 sprig fresh thyme
1 cinnamon stick
1 ounce dark chocolate, finely grated
1 pound small new potatoes (if large cut in quarters), peeled

In a large casserole or Dutch oven heat the oil and sauté the bacon at low heat until browned all over. Remove with a slotted spoon and set aside.

Generously salt and pepper the lamb chops. Brown well on both sides at high heat, then remove and set aside.

Brown the onion, making sure it doesn't burn. Add the garlic and stir. Add the flour and cook for about 2 minutes. Add the sherry, broth, and ½ cup water and scrape the bottom of the pan.

Add the herbs, cinnamon, and chocolate and return the bacon to the casserole. Mix well, add the potatoes, and cook at low heat for about 20 minutes or until the potatoes are cooked through but not falling apart.

Return the lamb chops to the casserole, bathe with the sauce, and cook for about 3 minutes until heated through. Serve.

Mango Shortcakes

The mango shortcakes are a natural end to this meal. I have
made the dough a bit sweeter than normal because instead of
serving with whipped cream, I serve the shortcakes with light
sour cream, which makes a refreshing contrast. I have added pistachios for their texture and color, and since they are in the same
family as mangoes (along with cashews and poison ivy), it is a
natural segue.

For the Shortcakes
3 cups all-purpose flour
4½ teaspoons baking powder
⅓ cup sugar
½ teaspoon salt
10 tablespoons unsalted butter, very well chilled
1 cup whole milk, chilled
1 cup chopped pistachios

To Assemble
3 to 3½ cups ripe diced mangoes (3 to 4 mangoes, about 3 pounds)
¾ cup mango puree*
1¼ cups light sour cream

> **To make the mango puree, blend 1 ripe, very sweet mango, 1 tea-
> spoon brown sugar, and 1 to 2 teaspoons lime juice in a blender.
> In a pinch, you can substitute mango marmalade.*

Preheat the oven to 425°F. Sift the flour and baking powder together into a bowl, add the sugar and salt, and stir to mix.

Cut the butter into small pieces and incorporate into the flour mixture by taking a big pinch of the ingredients and rubbing together. Do this until the mixture is the consistency of coarse cornmeal. Make a well in the center of the dry ingredients and add the milk and ⅔ cup of the chopped pistachios. Mix with your hand just until the flour is completely moistened and the ingredients form a loose dough. If overmixed, the dough will be tough.

Pat out the dough onto a floured surface and pat down until the dough is about ¾ inch thick. Cut the dough into eight circles (or any shape you like, stars, for example) using a floured, sharp-edged biscuit or cookie cutter or knife. Do not use a glass. The dull edge will pinch the top and bottom together and the biscuits will not rise properly. If the thickness of the dough does not allow eight circles, reassemble and reroll only once. The more you handle the dough the tougher it will get!

Place the shortcakes on a silicone baking mat or an ungreased cookie sheet and bake for 10 to 12 minutes. The biscuits should double in height and color very lightly. Remove from the oven and allow to cool on a rack.

Do not assemble the shortcakes ahead of time; do so just as you are ready to serve. You might even want to heat the shortcakes very slightly.

Split the biscuits by pulling them apart. On each of the bottom halves of the biscuits place 2 or 3 tablespoons of the diced mango, drizzle with 1 or 2 teaspoons of the mango puree, and top with a generous tablespoon of sour cream. Place the remaining biscuit halves on top, then a little sour cream and more mango, then pour about a tablespoon of the mango puree on top of each. Sprinkle on the remaining chopped pistachios to finish, and serve.

4

AFTER
THE REVOLUTION

TWENTY-SIX

January 1, 1959

At three A.M. thunderous pounding on our front door and a loud voice calling our names awakened us from deep sleep. It was Guillermo Cabrera Infante, the writer. Fidel had come down from the Sierra Maestra, Camilo Cienfuegos had taken Santa Clara in Las Villas province, and Batista had fled the country. We opened another bottle of champagne for Kir Royales and toasted the victory of the Revolution.

Roberto and Guillermito were rejoicing, discussing a future rich in possibilities and new liberties and looking forward to the release from jail of some of their friends, their only offense having been painting revolutionary slogans on walls. They talked for some time before Guillermo decided to leave. He needed to find out how the situation was being officially handled and he needed to go home to his family. Wanting to contribute in some way I made a really strong *café con leche* and we ate the mango short-cakes that had been left over from the night before.

None of us thought it would be dangerous to be out on the street. But it was. From our front window we started to see policemen and soldiers still in their uniforms wandering aimlessly, not quite knowing where to go or what to do. We could see that the *bodega* hadn't opened and neither had any of the neighborhood stores. We saw some punches thrown, heard guns going off and what looked like the beginning of a riot. We closed the window, but we couldn't see much—Boy Scouts directing traffic, groups of men here and there, spontaneous manifestations in favor of Fidel. The number of rumors that reached us through neighbors was dizzying. Fidel had flown to Havana, no, he had not. Batista took sacks of dollars and gold, no, he had been "detained" before he could leave. There was no way to tell fact from wishful thinking.

Roberto and I were anxious for solid news. He reached his mother on the phone, but she couldn't see much from her window either. I couldn't sit still. Where was my brother Clive? Still in the mountains with the guerillas? Was Papi all right? Was Tío Trampo at home? Was Mami alone? I knew my brother Aubrey was safe, as he and his wife had had no plans to go out. I finally managed to reach everyone by phone and was assured everyone was okay. But I was still jumpy.

I tried to calm down by cooking. I had gone grocery shopping a couple of days before and there was plenty of food in the house. I wanted to cook until I got tired and then invite the neighbors over for some soothing food.

Kir Royale

1 part crème de cassis
5 parts very cold brut champagne

Pour the crème de cassis in a champagne goblet or flute and slowly pour the champagne on top.

Serves 1.

Pollito en Cazuela
(Stewed Whole Chicken)

Mami made this dish in times of stress. It has a soothing quality, maybe due to its intoxicating aroma. Serve with plain white rice or coconut rice

> One 3- to 3½-pound chicken
> Salt and freshly ground black pepper to taste
> 2 tablespoons olive oil
> 1 large onion, chopped
> 1 tablespoon flour
> 6 garlic cloves, sliced
> 1 teaspoon finely minced fresh thyme
> 1 teaspoon finely minced fresh oregano
> 2 bay leaves
> 1 stick cinnamon (the magic in this dish)
> ½ cup Spanish dry sherry
> ½ cup chicken broth

Rinse the chicken and dry well, removing all visible fat. Refrigerate overnight uncovered. This will dry the skin and allow to brown better.

When ready to cook, salt and pepper the chicken. Heat the oil in a Dutch oven and brown the chicken well on all sides. Remove the chicken.

Add the onion and brown well for a good color. Sprinkle with flour, scrape the bottom of the pan (this will slightly thicken the juices), and add the rest of the seasonings, sherry, and broth. Stir.

Bring to a boil and return the chicken to the pot. Reduce the heat, cover, and let simmer for 1½ hours, turning the chicken on a different side every half hour. I know it sounds like too long, but that is the beauty of it—the meat should be falling off the bones.

Turn off the heat, cut the chicken in quarters and place on a serving platter. Pour the cooking juices over the chicken without straining. Serve.

Arroz con Coco
(Coconut Rice)

When a Cuban wants to express bewilderment he asks himself, *"¿Como le entra el agua al coco?"* "How does the water get inside the coconut?" On January 1, 1959, we were bewildered, to say the least. This intriguing coconut rice, not so well known in Havana, was a specialty of one of my mother's half sisters, who still lived in Manzanillo in Oriente province where Mami was born. This recipe calls for both coconut water and coconut milk.

> 1 cup long-grain rice
> 1¼ cups coconut water (fresh or canned)
> 1 teaspoon salt
> 1 tablespoon olive oil or butter
> ½ cup unsweetened coconut milk (not piña colada mix)
> ⅓ cup unsweetened coconut flakes

Put the rice in a colander and rinse under running water until the water is clear. Put in a heavy pot, add the coconut water, salt, and oil and bring to a boil. The moment the rice comes to a boil, add the coconut milk, cover tightly, and turn the heat down to a simmer. Cook without disturbing for 15 to 20 minutes. Uncover, add the coconut flakes, fluff with a fork, and taste the rice for doneness. It should be firm but not underdone. (If you think it needs more cooking time, sprinkle a little water on the rice and continue cooking for 3 to 5 minutes). After fluffing the rice turn the heat off, cover again, and allow to rest for 10 minutes over the hot burner. Fluff before serving.

TWENTY-SEVEN

The New Order

My only compass in life had always been the idea of fairness, simple fairness, to yourself and to others. What was going on all around me after Fidel came to power was far from fair. I did not like it.

With the promise of democratic elections Fidel had gained wide support, but almost immediately, even before he reached Havana, a cry went out: *"¿elecciones? ¿para qué?"* Elections, what for? Castro was the one and only man who could head the nation. Our illusion of a return to democracy was quickly shattered. Civil liberties were curtailed and *milicianos* and neighborhood watchdogs took over. Every parcel you carried in or out of a building had to be inspected. The press exercised self-censorship and our daily lives changed so quickly I could not absorb the reality of our new circumstances fast enough.

January 2: Fidel calls for a general strike.

January 3: Castro declares Santiago the capital of Cuba in recognition of the support, moral and physical, Oriente province had always given him. Only to revert himself soon after.

January 5: The constitution of 1940, with its liberal and democratic nature and policies regarding welfare and unemployment, is amended and the power passed from the presidency to the council of ministers.

January 10: The death penalty is established and private property is seized by the government if deemed that "political crimes" have been committed.

January 30: Constitutional warranties and *habeas corpus* are rescinded.

February 7: The *Ley Fundamental,* fundamental law, is established and the constitution of 1940 is revoked.

Revolutionary courts are established and begin conducting summary trials ending in the same verdict, guilty. The sentence was from twenty to life in abominable prison conditions. With the attitude of shoot first, ask questions later, several hundred men convicted on specious charges are shot point blank, their backs to the wall in the courtyard of La Cabaña. (La Cabaña was a military fortress that sat across the bay from the city, situated right next to the Morro Castle—both the most beautiful and emblematic buildings of colonial times, built to protect the entrance to the bay and defend the city of La Habana.) Che Guevara becomes supreme prosecutor in La Cabaña, willing to torture, jail, or execute any dissident—not just Batista goons or members of the military forces, but civilians too. It's pure vengeance, carried out with the conceit of eliminating all possibility of a counterrevolution.

In March, Soviet state "technicians" and "advisors" begin arriving. You can easily tell who they are by their red faces full of perspiration and their inappropriate clothing for the tropics.

Their specialty is security and they have been invited to Cuba with the express purpose of helping to establish a police state society. The idea is to engender a climate of guilt; everyone is guilty of something, so anybody is subject to arrest at any time, a popular dictum in all totalitarian regimes.

You cannot criticize the government, or the *milicianos,* or the neighborhood sympathizers. Not only are you prohibited to dissent, but you are forced to be enthusiastic about Fidel and demonstrate passion for anything he does or says. If you aren't fully with Fidel, waving your little flag, you are against him and subject to closer scrutiny. Anyone can accuse you of anything, including owning property or working for an American corporation. It makes you "socially dangerous" or a *gusana,* a worm, the epithet reserved for counterrevolutionaries and the bourgeoisie. The *gusano* accusation always comes as a threat, as if to taunt you into action. It is frightening. There is the very real danger of being arrested at any moment and having the G2 (secret military police) make a case against you.

April 5: Amid the grumbles of the labor union members, always a strong force in Cuba, the leadership of the *Confederación de Trabajadores Cubanos* revokes the right to strike because "strikes are no longer necessary."

June 13: In a massive public rally Fidel denounces anyone critical of the *Reforma Agraria* (the agrarian reform) as "traitors."

July 7: Law #425 is approved, defining all criticism of the government's reforms or declaring oneself anti-Communist as a "counterrevolutionary crime." (Fidel does not admit to being a Communist himself until after the Bay of Pigs battles.)

Ajiaco
(Mostly Vegetable Stew)

Known throughout the Americas as *sancocho,* this dish is claimed by every Latin country as the true and only one. In fact, there are as many versions of the dish as there are pots. The origins of the *ajiaco* in Cuba go as far back as our native Indians (who the Spanish annihilated), when it was most likely just a simple vegetable stew. Out of necessity due to the shortages in Havana, I went back to the stew's original purity and made it with vegetables only. Before the Revolution, as the dish had become popular over time and with prosperity, different types of meat had been added to the stew. This recipe is one of those versions for more prosperous times.

The good thing about this type of dish is that you need not be a slave to the recipe. Improvising is encouraged. Follow the steps and don't be afraid to mix them up and don't feel daunted by the list of ingredients—it really is an easy dish to make. You can substitute potatoes and carrots for a couple of the tropical tubers (doesn't much matter which). Use the semiripe plantains if you can (they provide a pleasant sweetness), or substitute *calabaza,* the orange-yellow Caribbean pumpkin.

For the sofrito
3 tablespoons olive oil
1 large onion, minced
1 red bell pepper, minced
6 garlic cloves, minced
1 beef bouillion cube, crumbled

For the Meats

1 pound fatty short ribs or brisket
1 pound chicken thighs, cut in half
1 teaspoon salt
½ teaspoon freshly ground black pepper

For the Vegetables

2 ears of corn, cut in 1-inch rings
2 small to medium malangas, or 2 potatoes, peeled and cut into 1-
    inch slices
1 small to medium boniato, peeled and cut into 1-inch slices (op-
    tional)
1 medium-ripe plantain (yellow with no black spots), peeled and cut
    into 1-inch slices

To Finish

Grated zest of 2 lemons
3 garlic cloves, minced
½ cup minced parsley

To make the sofrito, the flavor base of the dish, heat the oil in a large Dutch oven or casserole, add the onion and bell pepper, and sautée until soft. Add the garlic and bouillion cube and stir so that you break up the cube.

Add the meats, season with salt and pepper, and stir to coat with the sofrito. Add 10 to 12 or more cups water, enough to cover the meats by 1½ inches, bring to a boil, and lower the heat. Simmer and skim until the broth is clear. This process will take several minutes but is essential for looks and taste. Cook at low heat for about 2 hours or until the meats are fork tender.

Add the corn, *malangas*, and *boniato* and cook for 10 to 15 minutes. Add the plantain and cook for an additional 15 minutes or until soft but not falling apart. If there is not enough broth in the pot to cover the vegetables, cook them separately in salted water. Drain well and add the cooked vegetables to the meats. Stir to mix.

Adjust the seasoning. Combine the lemon zest with garlic and parsley and sprinkle on top, or simply add the juice of 2 lemons. Serve all together in large bowls, or serve the broth first, then meats and vegetables on a plate.

TWENTY-EIGHT

Papi Is Arrested

In 1960 during one of Fidel's long public harangues, Papi was arrested at his home. A dozen *milicianos* stormed in and tore his place apart. My dad was taken by complete surprise and couldn't imagine why he had been targeted or what they were looking for.

By coincidence I arrived in the middle of the plunder bearing a mango pie, my father's favorite. I had baked it that morning. I must have looked as perplexed and frightened as my dad because one of the *milicianos* took me aside to tell me that among other things, my father was being investigated for growing a beard. "For growing a beard?" "Yes, to pass himself off as a *miliciano* and get physically close enough to Fidel to assasinate him." (The *milicianos* were also called *"barbudos"* for the beards they had grown in the mountains with Fidel.) I giggled nervously at the absurdity of the accusation.

My dad had cultivated a short, well-defined beard—the disputed item—since his twenties. He had grown it to hide the weakness of his chin. This small conceit was to cost him three years in a Castro prison.

Papi had hundreds of books on shelves, stacks on the floor, on his desk, everywhere. While he and I watched in stunned silence, holding each other by the waist, the *milicianos* rifled the pages of each and every one. A very tired five-dollar bill slowly flew in a zigzag out of an old magazine and gently fell to the floor. No doubt a long forgotten payment from a consultation that he had done by mail for one of his Central American clients. Now, in addition to the beard, he was accused of trading in *divisas,* foreign currency, a very grave offense at the time.

I could not believe this was happening. It was a scene from the theater of the absurd; it simply could not be real. But real it was, as Papi was dragged to the headquarters of the G2 secret police. I was the only one who had witnessed his arrest, but I had no idea what to do. When my soul finally returned to my body, I called my Tía Teresa, who was a friend of Celia Sánchez, Fidel Castro's right hand.

Celia couldn't do anything (or wouldn't do anything), so for two weeks I sat on a bench on the porch of the house that was now converted into G2 headquarters. I was not allowed to enter. No one would speak to me or give me any news of my father. At the end of the two weeks, one of the *milicianos* casually told me Papi had been transferred to a prison but he didn't know where.

I saw my father two or three months later. He was being held at La Cabaña fortress, the scene of the many shootings that took place at the very beginning of the Castro regime, awaiting trial.

To visit my father I had to take the *lanchita,* the same small rickety ferry I had once taken with Dulce to see the Virgen de Regla in happier times. The *lanchitas* I had once loved, with their bright-colored awnings and sassy sway, were already faded, broken down, cheerless, and even dangerous for lack of maintainance.

The military checkpoint was at the top of a climb up a steep hill. It was a very hot windless day, the sun was high, and the blue waters of the bay offered no comfort. My walk to the top was slow, both from the heat and the deep sadness I was feeling. I was carrying some candy and a bag of fruit for Papi. The *miliciano* at the checkpoint took one bite out of each banana, orange, and apple to make sure nothing was concealed. To further humiliate me, and punish my father, he conducted a very thorough strip search. I remained soberly silent and tearless.

I had to stand another hour in the sun before I was allowed to climb the last stretch to La Cabaña. I went into a cavernous room where prisoners waited for a decision to be made about them. Someone called out my father's name and a thin, clean-shaven man sitting on a cot two feet in front of me answered. It was my Papi. I had not recognized him. This time I cried.

Mango Pie

1 round Pillsbury pie dough
1 cup whole milk
3 egg yolks
½ cup sugar
¼ cup flour
¾ cup toasted almond flour*
3 drops (only) almond extract
2 large ripe mangoes, peeled and thinly sliced (about 2 cups)

*Roasted almonds milled to a fine meal. Can be found in gourmet shops or through bakers' catalogues, or can be made with unpeeled toasted almonds pulverized in the blender.

Stretch the round of dough over a French tart pan with a removable bottom or use a regular pie plate. Make a border, prick the dough with a fork, and bake blind (with no filling) according to the package instructions. Remove from the oven and allow to cool.

Place the milk in a saucepan and heat to boiling. Remove from the heat before it spills.

Beat the yolks and sugar in a bowl with a whisk or electric mixer until pale yellow and thick. Add the flour and mix well. Pour the milk into the mixture and mix well. Pour back into the saucepan, return to the stove, and cook over medium heat while stirring until the mixture is thick and smooth.

Turn off the heat, add the almond flour and stir vigorously. Add the extract and stir. Allow to cool. When both the pie dough and almond cream are cool, evenly spread the cream on the pie. Starting at the edges, overlap slices of mango while moving toward the center to make an attractive design.

TWENTY-NINE

Deceit

By early 1960, the promises Fidel had made to us as a people had completely vanished. More private property was being confiscated, especially that belonging to American companies. Since 1958, the U.S. firms had been diversifying away from the large sugar plantations and into utilities. By 1960 Fidel had nationalized all public services, effectively implementing an urban reform as he had done with the agrarian reform. The farmers had not gotten the land they had been promised and now worked in government cooperatives. The clerks in utility companies now worked for nationalized companies. It meant they all had the same boss, the Castro government.

There was no longer any pretense of a free press or unions and all other organizations were being controlled at the highest levels. The old guard of the Communist party in Cuba was more visible in important posts. Castro continued to deny he was a Communist, but it was becoming evident that we were heading toward a totalitarian regime. Russian "advisors" were everywhere.

There was an urban anti-Castro movement that began to pose threats to the government but in the end, even after taking enormous risks and making many sacrifices, it was ineffectual. The lack of organization and communication doomed the group even before Fidel could. One of Roberto's friends was at the fringes of the group and sadly Roberto had to tell him not to come to see us anymore. As much as we sympathized, our association with him was putting us in danger.

In October 1960, Washington banned exports to Cuba other than food and medicine, and serious shortages followed. The blockade had begun and it was immediately used (and it continues to be used) as an excuse to explain the lack of coffee and sugar, among most other things, in a country that had exported them for centuries.

One morning, shopping at the corner *bodega,* I ran through my usual list as I did every day. Onions? No. Garlic? No. Any vegetables? One tired plantain and a very skuzzy *malanga.* The regular sidewalk chicken cages and eggs had been gone for some time. Finally in desperation I asked the clerk to give me whatever he had. With a menacing look and foul humor, he handed me a can of seal meat from the Soviet Union. My eyes came out of my sockets and the expression on my face must have said it all because before I could say a word, he accused me of being *una gusana* and started berating me. It was alarming. That was the moment of my epiphany: We would have to leave Cuba.

In the meantime, I had to make do with whatever food we could find or barter. Eggs, sometimes, and whatever else we could scrounge from a neighbor who fished or the one who had relatives in the country. Our cousin América was genius at finding where they were selling any produce or meat, and would give me a call so I could join her in the queue before they ran out of whatever it was. Cooking had become a dodgy experience.

Escabeche
(Pickled Swordfish)

Recipes like this one come from the colonial era when there was no refrigeration. The fish could be held preserved with a fresh flavor for weeks in a tasty sauce of oil and vinegar, peppers, onions, and spices. It was placed in a well-covered glazed clay *cazuela* and kept in a cool place. Although there are many, many versions of this dish the principle recipe hasn't changed that much, just the preserving. I use a sterilized wide-mouth jar. It will keep fresh in the fridge for up to three or four weeks.

The *escabeche* is perfect for a light lunch served with a salad and good country bread, or for those times when you open the fridge not really knowing what you want to eat.

½ cup flour
1 teaspoon salt
2 pounds swordfish sliced into ¾-inch steaks
2 cups really good Spanish olive oil
2 red onions, thinly sliced
2 green bell peppers, thinly sliced
½ Habanero chile,* minced
10 garlic cloves, smashed
6 bay leaves
1 tablespoon black peppercorns
2 cups white vinegar

*The Habanero chile is the hottest there is, ringing the bell at about 300,000 Scovilles. A hot chile is not traditional, but I think it gives the escabeche that good ol' Cuban zest. Be very careful not to touch your mouth or eyes after handling.

Combine the flour and salt and use to dust the swordfish steaks. Heat ½ cup of the oil in a large skillet over medium heat, brown the fish, and cook for 5 minutes on each side until completely done. Don't crowd the fish steaks in the pan; cook in several batches if necessary.

Remove the fish from the skillet and drain on paper towels. Do not discard the oil.

Add the remaining oil and the remaining ingredients. Cook at high heat for 2 minutes. Reduce the heat to low and simmer for about 5 minutes or until the vegetables are wilted but not thoroughly cooked. Remove from the heat and allow to rest for several minutes.

In a wide-mouth jar make layers with the fish and the vegetables and pour in the remains of the skillet to top. Close the jar and allow to cool completely before refrigerating.

Always serve at room temperature with a good squeeze of fresh lemon.

THIRTY

The Warrior

My brother Clive had graduated from the Air Force Academy under the Batista regime in 1957 or 1958. Immediately after graduation he left Havana to join the Castro rebel forces in the mountains. It was supposed to be a secret, but somehow I knew. Clive was a man of pure heart and high ideals, and he believed in the ideology Fidel had set forth in the historic speech *La Historia me Absolverá* (History Will Absolve Me), which he gave in self-defense during his trial in 1953. The impassioned speech was all about the need for fairness, about education and housing, about the need for democratic elections and for a government above reproach.

Castro and his men had been apprehended after their failed attack on the Moncada garrison in the city of Santiago in Oriente province on July 26, 1953. Fidel and a ragtag group of men had come from Mexico by boat for the sole purpose of starting an insurgency and deposing Batista. This attack on a military garrison marked the beginning of the Revolution.

We worried about Clive especially because we didn't hear from him very often. Mami had seen him once or twice during several trips she had made to the Sierra Maestra to deliver medicine and a few handguns. I had no idea she was involved in the *Movimiento 26 de Julio* and was oblivious to her militancy.

I had not seen Clive since his return to Havana from the Sierra Maestra. It has been my understanding he arrived in Havana during the first few days of January ahead of Fidel who arrived riding a tank on January 8th. We did not see Clive right away, in fact, we didn't see him for sometime. But he must have been in the Castro inner circle as he was made Captain and given a wide range of responsibilities.

When Clive was finally able to visit home, Mami made his very favorite dish, *tamal en cazuela,* a fresh corn casserole spiked with a pork stew. It wasn't just Clive's favorite, we all loved it, mostly because it was one of the few dishes Mami always made herself.

After that short home visit Clive became increasingly involved in the Revolution, with ever-growing responsibilities, so we didn't see him very often. In fact, the last time I saw him was a blur. He had come by Mami's apartment in a great hurry, very excited, looking for winter clothes, anything anybody had, a coat, a scarf, gloves, anything. A difficult task in the tropics, but the whole family was put into action and managed to find enough warm clothing to dress him. Clearly he was going someplace cold. He told us it was a secret mission and couldn't say where. This was in early 1959, when Castro was still promising elections and long before he had declared Cuba a Communist state. Clive and one other pilot were going to Czechoslovakia to buy MIGs and to learn how to fly them, preparing for a counterinsurgency or invasion, but we didn't learn this until much later.

There were many errors and many promises broken leading up to and during the Cuban exile invasion. On April 17, 1961, in the Bay of Pigs, Clive flew in the defining battle. The MIGs had only just arrived in Cuba and were not yet battle ready, but Castro was determined to prove Cuban aerial superiority with whatever planes hadn't already been destroyed in the first throes of the invasion. And he did. After the defeat of the invading forces, my brother was acclaimed as *Héroe de la Revolución*, but he never made it home after that, not even for a few hours.

I left Cuba six weeks after the invasion and I never saw Clive again. After courageously declaring to Raúl Castro that he was disappointed with the regime and how far they had diverted from the original principles, Clive fell from favor and was ultimately sent to prison. The official reasons for his arrest were insubordination and neglecting his duties. After his release, he received a sanction that forbade him to work in anything that had to do with aviation and suffered further humiliations and dishonors that not only debilitated him but his sons too. My brother finally made it to Miami in 1991 and died of a massive heart attack six months later. I was living in California at the time.

At Clive's funeral, one of the B-52 pilots, a former enemy, told me firsthand the story of the Bay of Pigs as he had experienced it. In a kind voice, filled with emotion, he told me how brave and gallant Clive had been in battle. He was a true warrior. I was proud.

Tamal en Cazuela

This was Clive's favorite dish and Mami was required to make it any time he was around. It is a very typical country meal, satisfying and full of flavors with all the elements of the classic Cuban *tamal* just short of being wrapped in corn husks and steamed. This is a lazy cook's version, but I think it is just as tasty as the original.

For the Fricasée

1 tablespoon vegetable oil
1½ pounds pork chunks★
1 teaspoon salt
½ teaspoon freshly ground black pepper
½ teaspoon hot pimentón or paprika
2 large tablespoons sofrito★★
½ cup tomato sauce
2 tablespoons alcaparrado★★★
1 tablespoon white vinegar

For the Corn

6 cups frozen corn (two 1-pound bags, defrosted)
4 tablespoons (½ stick) unsalted butter
1 teaspoon sugar
Pinch of salt

★*This recipe also works well with boneless, skinless chicken chunks, but be sure to use only dark meat; the white will be too dry. Remember to adjust the cooking time—chicken pieces will take 25 to 30 minutes to cook.*

**If you don't feel like making a sofrito from scratch you can use bottled; there are a few acceptable brands on the market. To make from scratch, (p. 99).*

***Alcaparrado is a combination of capers and pimento-stuffed olives and is sold in jars.*

Heat the oil in a heavy skillet or Dutch oven. Season the meat with very little salt and pepper. Brown the pork chunks in the hot oil, then lower the heat and add pimentón, the sofrito, tomato sauce, alcaparrado, and vinegar. Stir to coat the meat, lower the heat, and cover and simmer for about 1 hour and 30 minutes or until the pork is tender.

Place the corn in a food processor in batches and pulse to make a coarse puree. Melt the butter in a second heavy skillet; add the corn, sugar, and salt. Cover and cook over very low heat for about 30 minutes, stirring often. When the pork is cooked, add it and its cooking juices to the corn. Stir to mix well. Serve.

THIRTY-ONE

Exodus

On April 17, 1961, when the shooting stopped at the Bay of Pigs, Fidel finally declared himself a Communist, an association he had denied vehemently since July 26, 1953 and the attack on the Moncada garrison.

First the canned seal meat and now Communism? Not so much that I was against a somewhat socialist society—there needed to be more justice, less disparity between the very poor and the very rich—but I was definitely against any kind of totalitarian rule. There was no time to waste getting out of Cuba. The exodus began and gained momentum each day as more of the professional and middle class population escaped.

There was no more waiting for a miracle. The miracle had made shore and been blown to smithereens. Roberto and I set about leaving right away and immediately turned to getting our papers in order. The paperwork to leave Cuba was daunting, but the most important document to have was a current passport and a U.S. visa, without which you were stuck in an indeterminate state for an indeterminate amount of time. At the same time, flights out of Havana were scarce and it was extremely difficult to get a reservation.

My first call was to Graziella, my childhood friend. Her parents owned a travel agency and she worked with them. We knew she would do anything she could to help us.

I myself had a valid passport and a U.S. multiple entry visa, but Roberto didn't. The rest of the documents were mostly releases from the Castro government, a letter from your place of work stating you were not needed, a release from an official stating you were not socially dangerous or a threat to the State, and a detailed inventory of all your possessions to the very last minutia, a search conducted and signed off by another low-level government official or a *miliciano*. Then, and only then, could you apply for an exit permit.

It was clear Roberto would not be able to leave with me. Not only did he lack a visa but his job at the Universidad de La Habana was considered essential. (With all the *milicianos* attending lectures, he had to make a rule that they couldn't bring firearms into the classroom—not a popular move.) My leaving was going to make everything that much harder for him, and if he stayed in our neighborhood he was going to be under constant scrutiny. He decided that once I left, he would go live with his mother until I could claim him through the visa waiver system that had been established by the United States.

Those were harrowing days. We were even afraid to speak in our apartment. We couldn't afford to make the smallest complaint or negative comment in case a neighbor was listening.

About a month after the Bay of Pigs and Fidel's declaration, I received a call from Graziella. She thought she might have a cancellation on a flight to Miami in the next few days, and if all my required paperwork was in order, she would move me up the list, but I had to be ready to leave within a moment's notice.

On May 17, Graziella called me again, this time with the news that she indeed had a cancellation and could book my flight for

May 20. If I didn't take that flight she could not foresee when she would be able to book me again.

Those last three days were the worst of all. I really did not have much time for good-byes, but I didn't want to leave Havana without seeing Graziella. We had been best friends since we were eight years old (and still are) and met in school over a plate of almond cookies. We loved to go to restaurants together and we always went to each other's family parties (and still do). Our relationship embraced our love of food and each other.

I wanted to prepare one last meal for her before I left. I wanted to invite her to dinner to thank her for everything, to say farewell. I didn't know when I would ever see Graziella, my husband, my family, or any of my friends again.

Through a few tricks, favors, and black market maneuvers, I managed to get enough ingredients to make some of Graziella's favorite dishes. Not the roast chicken she adored (I couldn't find a whole chicken), but I found shrimp and rice, green plantains, and enough eggs, milk, and flour to make the vanilla custard and almond cookies we both loved so much. These were our "Rosebud."

Enchilado de Camarones con Coco (Spicy Shrimp with Coconut Milk)

Easy and fast to make—perfect for a dinner party.

> 3 tablespoons olive oil
> 1 onion, minced
> 1 red bell pepper, diced
> 1 small Habanero chile, seeded and minced (or less to taste)
> 3 garlic cloves, minced
> 1 ripe tomato, diced
> 2 tablespoons tomato paste
> ¾ cup unsweetened coconut milk
> 1 pound medium shrimp, cleaned and shelled
> Salt and freshly ground black pepper to taste
> Minced parsley or cilantro for garnish

Heat the oil in a large skillet and add the onion, bell pepper, Habanero chile, and garlic. Stir and cook over medium heat until soft, about 5 minutes. Add the tomato and tomato paste and stir again. Add the coconut milk and stir, mixing well, until the coconut milk is heated through. Add the shrimp and stir to coat. Add the salt and pepper. Transfer to a serving dish and sprinkle with minced parsley. Shrimp should not cook more than 3 or 4 minutes.

Polvorones
(Dusty Almond Cookies)

The *polvorones* had always been "our" dessert. Light and pretty, dusted with confectioners' sugar and dressed in tissue paper. To us they were perfect for any occasion, great for breakfast with our *café con leche*, for a snack with a small glass of sweet sherry or port, with a simple vanilla custard (a Graziella thing) or our *cafecito* to finish the meal. These cookies are very fragile, making them that much more special. Wrapping them in tissues helps avoid their crumbling.

> 1 cup all-purpose flour
> 1 cup blanched almonds
> 8 tablespoons (1 stick) unsalted butter, softened
> ½ cup granulated sugar
> 1 small egg, slightly beaten
> ¼ teaspoon ground cinnamon (or more to taste)
> Pinch of salt
> Confectioners' sugar

Heat the oven to 350°F. Spread out the flour on a cookie sheet and toast until it begins to color, about 8 minutes. Transfer to a bowl. Toast the almonds in the oven until they are browned about 4 to 5 minutes. Process to make a coarse powder in a food processor or blender and combine with the flour.

In an electric mixer, cream the butter and sugar until all the grittiness of the sugar disappears. Add the egg and continue to cream. Add the flour and powdered almond mixture, cinnamon, and salt. Mix well. The dough will be rather sticky. Shape into a slightly flattened circle, cover with plastic, and chill for about 1 hour.

When ready to bake, preheat the oven to 300°F. Pinch off small amounts of the dough and roll into balls about 1 inch in circumference. Place the balls on a buttered baking sheet or a silicone baking mat, leaving about 2 inches between each. Bake 25 to 30 minutes or until they begin to color lightly. Do not brown.

Remove to a cooling rack. Dust with confectioners' sugar on both sides while still warm. Repeat when cookies have cooled and carefully wrap each cookie in tissue paper.

Makes 2 dozen.

THIRTY-TWO

Adiós La Habana — Hello Miami

The last few hours in the Havana airport were filled with anxiety. I was sad to leave but glad, terrified at the thought of being alone, but excited to be on my own. There was also the constant fear you could be stopped from leaving by a soldier or a *miliciano* at any point of the process. You'd never know if you were in the clear until you were aloft and past the boundaries of international waters.

I didn't want to look suspicious—of what I don't know—but I certainly did not want to call attention to myself. The *milicianos* had all the power and total discretion over what you would be allowed to take with you. This meant hours at the airport waiting for everyone's luggage to be examined, and for almost every person to be searched. Medals of saints worn for protection as well as wedding bands, even as simple as my own gold band, were confiscated.

After I was searched, I was left with only the clothes on my back and one five-dollar bill. A periwinkle linen suit, my famous Tropicana black pumps, and the black purse I had borrowed from my cousin Lourdes. That was all.

Everywhere around me people were crying and praying.

Everyone was distressed at leaving everything behind and having to face the immense unknown in front of us.

Stripped of my wedding band and my luggage, I arrived at the Miami airport on May 20, 1961, ironically the 59th anniversary of Cuba's Independence Day.

Would it be possible to return home soon? When would Roberto be able to join me? And my mother, what about her? Who was going to visit my father in prison? I waited at the airport for a friend of my mother's to pick me up, deep in thought and wondering what life would bring me now. Once we arrived at her apartment I felt grateful but I also felt caged.

How was I going to manage alone? What would I do? I would have to work, but how? I didn't know how to do anything. It was quite frightening facing a new life I knew so little about. My only outings (no one had a car) were to go to the Refugee Center to straighten out papers and ask for help. For the first time in my life, I had to figure out how to survive on my own.

Sadness and nostalgia engulfed me. We exiles lived with the illusion of returning to Cuba soon but even if that were to happen, I knew in my heart that nothing would be the same. There had been too many changes already. The Havana of my youth had been a unique place in time and space that would never be recovered again.

Papas con Chorizo (Potatoes with Chorizo)

Upon arriving in Miami as asylum seekers we had to complete another batch of papers before we could receive government aid, a little bit of money and surplus food. Every month we were given many pounds of Spam, a military-size can of powdered eggs, and an enormous log of processed cheese. These delicacies were not staples in a Cuban diet and not too much to our liking. We were grateful, and in awe of the generosity of this country. We weren't complaining. I simply could not swallow the eggs. I ran out of ways of cooking Spam, so I was pretty much on a cheese sandwich diet and soon returned to my pre-wedding weight of 94 pounds.

Roberto and I used to go to the supermarket to window-shop, to salivate over steaks and whole chickens. When we got our small check at the first of the month, I shopped for chorizo (not so easy to find in 1961 in Miami) and potatoes. I liked this little dish then for its flavors of home, and I still like it now.

1 tablespoon olive oil
1 cup minced onion
4 garlic cloves, minced
5 ounces Spanish chorizo, thinly sliced
2 cups potatoes, peeled and diced
Pinch of hot or smoky pimentón
4 tablespoons white wine or water
Salt

Thin slices of French bread, brushed with olive oil and toasted until crisp
Chopped parsley

Heat the oil in a skillet and sauté the onion until soft. Add the garlic and chorizo. Mix well and cook over medium heat until the chorizo has rendered some fat.

Add the potatoes and stir to coat. Add the pimentón and 2 tablespoons of the white wine. Cover slightly and cook over medium-low heat, stirring occasionally, for about 20 minutes.

Add the remaining wine and stir to coat. Cover loosely and cook over low heat for another 10 to 15 minutes until the potatoes are done. Sprinkle with a little salt. Place the toasted bread over the potatoes, dust with parsley, and serve from the skillet, or place a manly deep fried egg on top.

Epilogue

Roberto arrived in Miami two or three months after I did. With help from the Cuban Refugee Center we rented an apartment in the then decrepit neighborhood of South Beach. It was the cheapest we could find. We entertained ourselves by going window shopping at the grocery store and spent our days in the air-conditioned library or the 25-cent triple-feature movie house.

Through the Refugee Center Roberto found a job teaching in the middle of the Bible Belt in Arkansas but without friends or family support, the marriage didn't last long. He eventually moved to the East Coast and taught at exclusive women's colleges as a professor of Latin American literature. He married twice more.

My brother Aubrey and his growing family settled in Miami. My mother made it out of Cuba first to live in Miami and then to follow me to Manhattan. Papi died in an asylum, still a prisoner. Pupen stayed in Cuba, and I was never able to establish contact with her. Graziella came to the States, had five children, is still married to the man she married at seventeen, and we still speak every day. Guillermo Cabrera Infante established himself in London and went on to win many literary prizes. Before his death in 2005, he wrote, with actor Andy García, the screenplay for the film *The Lost City,* set in Havana in the late fifties.

I became a flight attendant, managed a year at Le Cordon Bleu cooking school in Paris, and later got a bachelor's degree from Fordham University in New York. Later still, there were several courses of regional cooking in Spain. I traveled a lot, married and divorced again, and traveled some more, taking away food memories and adventure from every place I visited. Writing about those experiences I became a food writer.

Neither Roberto nor I ever had children.

I have never returned to Havana. For now, it lives on in my enduring memories and in my dreams.

Acknowledgments

My first thanks have to go to the memory of my mother and father, Sylvia Molé Betancourt and Carlos Carballo Romero, for living life so fiercely and unconventionally, and to all my satellite parents: my beloved godmother, Fulgencia Santana, who enchanted me; Dulce, our cook, who taught me about Changó and Yemayá and their favorite foods; Kiki, who spoiled me beyond reason; Don Juan *el carpintero*, Doña Pastorita, and Ramón *el apuntador* for enriching my childhood; and to Tía Patria and Cousin América for teaching me to cook *a la Cubana*. Thanks to Mrs. Prieto, my first-grade teacher at Ruston Academy, for teaching me how to read and write and for making me think I was the "teacher's pet." I thank all my teachers past and present for trying to extract from me the best I could give. My everlasting gratitude and respect to all my Buddhist teachers for making me aware that the only goal worth having, is developing a heart of loving kindness.

I thank my schizophrenic Tía Berta, my senile Abuela Doña Monona, and my deaf Tío Octavio for demonstrating that perfection is seriously overrated. I also thank the memory of my brother Douglas Rudd for his valor, and for being loyal to his ideals in spite of the tragic reality of the Revolution.

I thank my nephew and nieces in the States, Argentina, Sweden, and Spain, obvious victims of the Cuban Diaspora, and their curiosity about the Havana that has moved me to write this book in the first place. I also thank my brother George Rudd and my cousins Leonor Carballo Bedevia and Silvia Molé García for helping me remember.

My childhood friend Graziella Martínez Cora, the tortoise to my hare, deserves my thanks for her good advice, steadfast love, and unconditional support all through our lives and for the fact that we still have the ability of cracking each other up every time we speak. I thank my long-time best friends Cathy Schwartz Voigts for always looking after my best interests and getting me through some very difficult moments; Louie Sloves, the ideal travel companion, who read every word of the manuscript at least ten times, for her good humor, her restless creativity, and her ability to always come up with new projects for us to try out, be it travel, recipes, or business ideas; Wendy Grace for trying very hard, but still failing, to teach me about style; and Wilma Espinoza, from California, for making me understand that beyond being Cuban I am a Latina woman.

I thank Chef Charles Narsés, who got me through Le Grand Diplôme at Le Cordon Bleu, Paris, long before going to cooking school became fashionable and even before I spoke French, with his regular reply of *Parce que çe comme ça,* Madame to any of my questions. It made me a better observer and his devoted student. In the chef category I would be remiss if I didn't mention my friends Aitor Elizegi from Bilbao, Angel Palacios from Barcelona, Edar Montero from New York, and Norman Van Aken in Miami for their generosity in allowing me to watch them work and explaining to me complex techniques and delicious recipes in intricate detail. I especially want to thank Sergio Navarro in Miami for brilliantly helping me test the recipes for this book, accompanied by much music and laughter.

My appreciation goes to Felicia Gressette, my first editor at the *Miami Herald,* for making me a better writer with her keen observations and her gentle prodding.

My thanks to Sharon Bowers for her encouragement and for introducing me to Katherine. My deepest gratitude goes to my agent, Katharine Cluverius at ICM, for her guidance from concept to proposal to finished manuscript and for finding the absolute best home for our baby, *Havana Salsa,* with Sarah Branham at Atria. Sarah, with her uncanny talent for asking the right questions, is what every writer wants, an editor that makes you seem a better writer than you really are.

Bibliography

BOOKS

Alfonso y Rodríguez, Dolores. *La cocina en el hogar.* New York: Minerva Books, 1963.

Barclay, Juliet. *Havana: Portrait of a City.* London: Cassell Illustrated, 2003.

Bolivar Aróstegui, Natalia, and Carmen Gonzalez Díaz de Villegas. *Mitos y leyendas de la comida afrocubana.* Havana: Editorial de Ciencias Sociales, 1993.

Cabrera Infante, Guillermo. *Tres tristes tigres.* Barcelona: Editorial Seix Barral, 1970.

Cabrera Infante, Guillermo. *La Habana para un Infante Difunto.* Barcelona: Editorial Seix Barral, 1979.

Cabrera, Lydia. *El monte.* Reprint, Miami: Ediciones Universal, 1995.

Calera, Ana Maria. *Cocina catalana.* Madrid: Editorial Everest, 1988.

Castellanos, Jorge, and Isabel Castellanos. *Cultura afrocubana: Las religiones y las lenguas.* Miami: Ediciones Universal, 1992.

Colegio Hebreo Sefaradí. *Comida Sefardí.* Mexico City: Servicios Litográficos Trujillo, 1986. http://www.mesianicos.com/comida/comida/htm.

Efundé, Agún. *Los secretos de la Santería.* Miami: Editorial Cubamérica, 1978.

Fagiuoli, Martino, ed. *Cuba.* San Diego: Thunder Bay Press, 2002.

Fernández, Frank. *L'anarchisme à Cuba.* Paris: Editions CNT, 2004.

Fernández, Santalices, Manuel. *Mis lugares preferidos en la Habana.* Madrid: Agualarga Editores, 1993.

Franqui, Carlos. *Camilo Cienfuegos*. Reprint, Barcelona: Editorial Seix Barral, 2002.

Friedman, Max Paul. *Nazis and Good Neighbors: The United States Campaign Against the Germans of Latin America in World War II*. Cambridge: Cambridge University Press, 2003.

Greene, Graham. *Our Man in Havana*. New York: Penguin Books, 1958.

Hart Phillips, R. *Cuba: Island of Paradox*. New York: McDowell, Obolensky, 1959.

Iglesias, Elena. *Cuenta el caracol*. Miami: Ediciones Universal, 1995.

Lachatañeré, R. *¡Oh, Mío Yemayá!!* Havana: Editorial de Ciencias Sociales, 1992.

Lachatañeré R. *El sistema religioso de los afrocubanos*. Havana: Editorial de Ciencias Sociales, 1992.

Lluriá de O'Higgins, María Josefa. *A Taste of Old Cuba: More Than 150 Recipes for Delicious, Authentic, and Traditional Dishes Highlighted with Reflections and Reminiscences*. New York: Morrow, 1994.

Madrinas de las Salas "Costales" y "San Martín" del Hospital Universitario "General Calixto García, eds." *¿Gusta, Usted? ¿Cómo cocinan los cubanos? Lo mejor de la cocina cubana*. Havana: Imprenta Uncal, 1956.

Morse, Kitty and Danielle Mamane. *The Scent of Orange Blossoms: Sephardic Cuisine from Morocco*. Berkeley: Ten Speed Press, 2001.

Palmer, Steven Paul. *From Popular Medicine to Medical Populism: Doctors, Healers, and Public Power in Costa Rica, 1800–1940*. Chapel Hill, NC: Duke University Press, 2003.

Parkinson, Rosemary, ed. *Culinaria the Caribbean: A Culinary Discovery*. Denmark: Konemann, 1999.

Pino, Rafael del *Amanacer en Girón*. Havana: Dirección Política de las Fuerzas Armadas Revolucionarias.

Raichlen Steven. *Miami Spice: The New Florida Cuisine*. New York: Workman, 1993.

Reyes Gavilán, María Antonieta. *Manual de cocina y reposteria*. Havana: Cultural S.A., 1952.

Rodríguez, Eduardo Luis. *La Habana, Arquitectura del siglo XX*. Barcelona: Blume, 1999.

Rout, Leslie B., and John F. Bratzel. *The Shadow of War: German Espionage and United States Counterespionage in Latin America during World War II.* ed. Thomas F. Troy. Bethesda, MA: University Publications of America, 1986.

Seuc, Napoleón. *La colonia china de Cuba, 1930–1960: Antecedentes, memorias y vivencias.* Miami: Ahora Printing, 1998.

Sternberg, Rabino Robert. *La cocina Sefardí: La riqueza cultural dela saludable cocina de los judíos mediterránea.* Barcelona: Editorial Zendrera Zariquiey, 1996.

Thomas, Hugh. *Cuba, or the Pursuit of Freedom.* New York: Da Capo Press, 1978.

Wolfe, Linda. *The Cooking of the Caribbean Islands.* New York: Little Brown & Co., 1970.

ARTICLES

Aragón, Uva, selected newspaper articles, *Diario de las Américas.*

WEB SITES

Alocubano.com.

Clark, Juan. "The Process of the Bay of Pigs," http://www.brigada2506.com/history.htm.

Encarta archives: 1938–1959.

Gangsters, Crimelibrary.com.

MIG 15 Fagot, Cubanaviation.com.

Mallin, Jay Sr. "Havana Nightlife: Sans Souci, World's Rawest Nightclub," http://www.cuban-exile.com/.

Perez, Juan Home Page, juanperez.com/#charada.

Project Muse—Cuban Studies, http://muse.jhu.edu/journals/cuban_studies/.

Punto de Bifurcación, Norbertofuentes.com.

Sierra, J.A., http://www.historyofcuba.com/cuba.htm.

Index